101 *salon* PROMOTIONS

BY ROBERT OPPENHEIM

MILADY

THOMSON LEARNING

Africa • Australia • Canada • Denmark • Japan • Mexico • New Zealand • Philippines
Puerto Rico • Singapore • Spain • United Kingdom • United States

NOTICE TO THE READER

Cover Design: Suzanne Nelson

Milady Staff:
Acquisitions Editor: Pamela Lappies
Project Editor: NancyJean Downey
Marketing Manager: Donna Lewis
Production and Art/Design Coordinator: Suzanne Nelson

Printed in Canada
4 5 6 7 8 9 10 XXX 04 03 02

For more information, contact Milady, 3 Columbia Circle, PO Box 15015, Albany, NY 12212-0515: or find us on the World Wide Web at http://www.Milady.com

Library of Congress Cataloging-in-Publication Data

Oppenheim, Robert, 1925-
 101 salon promotions / by Robert Oppenheim.
  p. cm.
 ISBN: 1-56253-358-4
 1. Beauty shops—Marketing. 2. Beauty shops—Management. I. Title.
TT965.O63   1999
646.72—dc21   98-4064
                                                 CIP

101
salon
PROMOTIONS

To Ruth

Contents

Section I: Seasonal

Section II: Holidays & Events

Section III: Networking

Section IV: Cut, Color, Nails

Section V: Retail, Parents/Kids

Section VI: Client Rewards & Coupons

Section VII: Miscellaneous Prep

OK, Here We Go. . . .

People who earn their livelihoods in the academic community—professors, department heads, instructors—are all familiar with a live-or-die guideline. "Publish or perish." They know that unless they do the research that results in published pamphlets, articles, or books, their careers drift sideways and ultimately shrivel.

We in the salon industry can paraphrase that guideline. In our case it would be: "*Promote* or perish." A salon cannot grow on a long-term basis, however well-appointed, clean, courteous, or populated with talented stylists. These will take a salon just so far and no further, and with competition increasing every day, stylists switching jobs, technology and techniques constantly changing, "just so far" won't be far enough. Every salon, from the biggest to the smallest and everything in between, including *your* salon, needs promotional activity to keep it going, keep it growing.

Years ago when I started lecturing on this subject, some hands would inevitably go up with the question, "Why do we have to promote? We are professionals. After all, doctors don't promote, dentists don't, lawyers don't." I don't get that question anymore, of course, because we're all familiar with the active and blatant advertising and promoting that these professions do. Accept it and ingest it. You must—*must*—promote your salon if your salon is to survive and grow.

Are you concerned that you won't be able to spare the funds needed for salon promotions? Never fear. Yes, you can always spend money, lots of it, with elaborate, complicated, glitzed-up promotions, but that's positively *not* what this book is all about. You'll find 101 different promotions in this book, but you won't find *any* that will cause a significant dent in your pocketbook. Quite the reverse. They can all be done *virtually on a shoestring*. So relax about the money thing. Even the expenses you do incur—for signs, for example, or printing, or maybe buttons, or cards—can often be obtained on a barter basis. The printing bill is $50? Perhaps the printer could be your guest for $50 worth of beauty services in exchange for $50 in printing services. Don't be reluctant to suggest this. More and more, small merchants are engaging in barter transactions.

It should also be said that promotions are nothing to be afraid of. Promotions aren't necessarily big, loud, colorful things. Neither are they necessarily complex and infinitely organized with precise recordkeeping. They *can* be all of these things, and that's fine if you're at ease with big, loud, colorful, and infinitely organized. Nothing wrong with any of that. But promotions can be the opposite, as well. They can be subtle or obvious, quiet or bombastic, hard sell or soft sell, complex or simple. Recordkeeping can be precise or relaxed.

There are dozens of types of promotions and dozens of variations on each type. How to sort them out? Don't be concerned. There are promotions that *will* be suited to *your* salon, *your* personality, *your* staff. From the 101 of them in this book, you won't have any trouble at all finding enough that will fit easily into your level of promotional comfort and ability.

A word about discounts, free goods, sampling, and the like. One school of thought says that it "cheapens" the salon. It does not! The most prestigious cosmetic line in the world is Estée Lauder. Mrs. Lauder found out decades ago that giving small sizes of products always was an automatic way to build business. Her competitors despised her for it, but they all got on the "gift-with-purchase" bandwagon. Restaurants? The best of them offer "prix fixe" dinners, which are nothing more than combo packages that combine several courses at a price lower than the total value of these courses. Lawyers? They work on "contingency" fees where their services are free if they don't win your case. Even plastic surgeons offer discounts if multiple procedures are done at the same time. The fact is that *everybody* engages in discounts, free goods, and sampling under one guise or another. It's part of the fabric of American business.

OK, now that all the fears, anxieties, and trepidations are put aside, here's what you should do, starting now. . . .

First and most important is read this book cover to cover, all 101 Promotions. Each promotion has tips, suggestions, philosophies, and ideas that will work for that specific promotion but that may very well be transferable to many other promotions. If you "cherry pick" just the promotions whose headlines intrigue you, you'll lose out on the underlying methodologies and techniques of other, related promotions whose concepts may easily translate to the promotions you're interested in. So please, *read this book cover to cover*.

I suggest that you don't go off and read the whole book all in one shot, or even in two or three sessions. If you do, the information will all kind of congeal and get blurry. Ideally you should read no more than five promotions at a time. Go through them slowly. Think about them. Visualize them in your salon. Then set the book down. If you're impatient and can't wait to get started, read ten—but no more. Tomorrow go through another five, maybe ten. In two or three weeks you will have gone through and thought about all 101 promotions. You will have given the promotions the thoughtful consideration that they merit. Your salon deserves no less.

Each promotion is numbered. If a promotion doesn't fit your salon's personality or doesn't seem suited to your clientele, simply pass it by. Go to the next promotion. It won't be long before you come across promotions that are right up your alley. Promotions where you feel, "That'll work." Promotions that you think are "cool." Promotions that excite you. Every time you come across one of these, jot down the number.

When you're done with this exercise, give the book to a couple of other people, and ask them to go through the same exercise. These folks can be your spouse, trusted stylists who know the personality and potential of your salon, or friends whose opinions your respect. Take your list and their lists of preferred promotions, and compare them. You'll surely find many that you all agree on. Perfect! You're going to pick the promotions you will actually be doing from this list that you've all selected.

Once you do get going with a promotional schedule, each promotional experience will give you valuable information as to what to do next. Every promotion will contain some elements that work beautifully and some elements that need improvement. Your accumulating experience will teach you what to improve, what to discard. It gets better and easier as it goes along.

Are there any lingering trepidations? Any reluctance because you think that promotions are somehow beneath your professional dignity? Take a look about you, open your mail, go through your newspapers, wander around your neighborhood. In the mail, in the papers, in store windows and, indeed, all over, you'll see promotional activity. You're surrounded by it. And the reason everyone does it is because it builds business. Now look in your own salon. Is each styling chair filled with a body each hour of the working week? No? That's reason enough to get promotional.

Professionalism? I love it, I espouse it, I encourage it, and you'll find nothing in this book that is unprofessional. On the other hand, empty chairs and idle stylists are indeed unprofessional. Let's keep those stylists busy. Let's keep those chairs filled.

Let's promote.

Each section in this book contains specific promotions grouped together by similarity. Many of them overlap, but this will provide a quick reference for you. Below is a listing of the icons that appear in this book and what they mean.

 Seasonal—promotions that have to do with a specific time of year or season

 Holidays—promotions tied to calendar holidays like Christmas and New Year's

Events—promotions that are focused on events like weddings and Monday-night football

 Networking—promotions that utilize the merchants around you and your best ways of working with them

 Cut—specifically designed to promote your cutting service

 Color—specifically designed to promote your coloring service

 Nails—specifically designed to promote your nail services

 Retail—promotions that help you increase your retail sales

 Parent/Child—promotions that are targeted to parents or children

 Client Rewards—promotions that offer clients rewards, things like receiving extra services for referring new clients

 Coupon—any promotion that uses a coupon given to clients

 Preparation Time—a promotion that requires some additional set up or preparation time in order to be effective

Discount—a promotion that offers discounted services

 Printed Materials—include brochures, mailings, cards, signs, postcards, etc.

 Miscellaneous—anything that doesn't fit into any category above

Acknowledgments

The publisher would like to thank the following professionals for their expertise in reviewing this manuscript: Darleen Hakola, Portland, OR; Victoria Harper, Kokomo, IN; Maren Lonergan, Davenport, IA; and Geri Mataya, Pittsburgh, PA.

Seasonal

Customer Crafts— A January Traffic Builder

What to do about January? The holiday season is over, folks may be a little short on cash, and most salons have plenty of empty space in the appointment book.

How well do you know your clients? Generally speaking, the relationship between client and hairstylist is closer than the relationship between the customer and virtually any other kind of retail or service store. To take advantage of this particular promotional idea, you've got to ask clients for some information, and you must start some months before the holiday season. You'll want to find out which of your clients, their immediate family members, other relatives, or friends are creative in a craft of some sort. You'll be amazed at how many of them have some particular talent they'd like to expose and hopefully sell. People make dolls, pin cushions, pottery, lampshades, carvings, and so on. If you've ever been to craft shows yourself, you know there is no end to the types of things that people work on, hobbies that people have.

1 When you've got yourself a list of people who have some sort of creative ability with a craft, call each one individually (you can write, but you'll get more participation if you call), inviting them to "exhibit" in your salon during the month of January.

2 You can exhibit as many different items as you have space available on counters, shelves, showcases, stations. Every piece you display should have a card, giving the name of the artist and the price of the piece. For your trouble, you ask for a mere 10 percent of the selling price. The crafts people will be delighted with your generosity because they would have to give a significantly higher percentage to a regular retailer who might carry their items. Your object is not to make money on the sales. Your object is to bring people into your salon during the month of January.

3 If it turns out that you are exhibiting the work of let's say, a dozen different people—some of them clients, some of them not—you will surely get each of those twelve people, plus all of their families and many of their friends and neighbors, into the salon to see the works "on exhibit"

YOUR OBJECT IS TO BRING PEOPLE INTO YOUR SALON DURING THE MONTH OF JANUARY.

in your "crafts show." That can translate into a couple of hundred people over the course of the month. Each of these people will not only see a display of crafts but also a clean, bright, happy salon with all sorts of beauty services taking place. That's the object of the whole exercise!

4 When they come in, looking around, walking around, and maybe purchasing a craft item or two, you can be sure that a significant percentage will talk to you as the owner, or to one of your stylists, about beauty services. They'll figure that if they can get a little bit of free advice, that's sort of a bonus for them. Yes, it is, but it's also your opportunity to sit them down in a chair, play with their hair a bit, suggest beauty services. Keep the selling soft. Less is more. By the end of January, you'll find you have made many new friends. It goes without saying that some of these new friends will become new clients.

5 Getting the word out on your "craft show" need not be an elaborate affair. Mostly you've got to invite every client who comes in during the Thanksgiving/Christmas/New Year period to: "Make sure you stop by in January. We're having a craft show right here in the salon." Between your putting the word out and the "exhibitors" putting the word out, you'll attract people.

6 If one of these craftspersons has a talent for art, as many do, you can ask her to make a cute sign saying CRAFT SHOW for your window. That's promotion enough. You don't want people flocking to the salon, you just want them ambling in, browsing about, seeing the salon, thanking you, and hopefully asking a beauty question or two.

Now isn't that much more fun than sitting around in an empty salon during the whole month of January? It sure is. And when you see the business that will result, you'll probably want to make it an annual affair.

YOU WANT PEOPLE AMBLING IN, BROWSING ABOUT, SEEING THE SALON, AND HOPEFULLY ASKING A BEAUTY QUESTION OR TWO.

April Showers Won't Ruin Your Hairstyle—If . . .

SEASONAL

PRINTED MATERIAL

Wash 'n wear hair has been with us for decades, but there are still countless women who absolutely *know* that if they go out in a shower, their hairstyle is gone. All these women would be instantly curious if they saw this sign in your window:

APRIL SHOWERS WON'T RUIN YOUR HAIRSTYLE . . .
IF YOU HAVE ONE OF OUR PRECISION WASH 'N WEAR CUTS

How could any woman resist if she has this kind of rainy-weather problem? You'll catch the attention of passersby who are clients of your competitors. They'll figure, "Maybe I ought to check this out. My stylist never told me about anything like this."

Obviously, you don't have to confine the message to just a sign in your window. Your salon may not even have a window. That's when you consider small ads in local newspapers or even neighborhood journals. Maybe you'll decide on postcards, in which case you should explain that your staff has the extra skills involved to analyze and precisely cut hair so that when it dries out after getting caught in a storm, the client only has to shake her head from side to side or fluff it up with her fingers and her hair is back to looking beautiful.

The perfect time to put the sign in the window or do the advertising or mail the postcards would be in the last week of March and through April. Countless conversations will take place during this period, all beginning, ending, or alluding to the fact that "April showers bring May flowers." And anytime a woman who has a cut that is not shower-resistant hears this cliché, she thinks, "Yeah, but those blasted April showers ruin my hairstyle."

By the time April is over, the promotion is over, too. So the risk that maybe it won't pay off is minimal and confined—but it *will* pay off. The key ingredient for success is how well your stylists can execute precision wash 'n wear cuts that will resist the elements.

If you make a promise in your advertising, you *must* deliver. If you're at all skeptical that your staff may really not have the technical skills to do this, don't risk this promotion, *but* you've got to see to it that everybody attains

THE KEY INGREDIENT FOR SUCCESS IS HOW WELL YOUR STYLISTS CAN EXECUTE PRECISION WASH 'N WEAR CUTS THAT WILL RESIST THE ELEMENTS.

these skills. This means going to classes and workshops, and it means lots of practicing.

Perhaps you or a friend or a particular stylist in the salon—have these wonderful technical skills. Fine, then you've got to schedule a couple of hours every week (either in the evenings, mornings, Sundays, or Mondays) to have that one person teach everybody else. Need heads to practice on? That'll be solved by running a couple of classified ads in your local newspaper offering free haircuts. (If you do advertise, make sure you say that if volunteers come in for their free haircut, it will be executed by a licensed hairdresser during advanced training sessions.)

When you've all acquired the skills, an April promotion will actually be secondary. The primary benefit you'll all have is greater confidence, enhanced professional self-esteem, and a desire to show off. Stylists will introduce the subject into their conversations with clients, they'll try to whet clients' appetites, and they'll succeed. Clients will be happier, staff will be happier, your haircut volume will increase—*then* you can run your April Showers promotion to lure new people in.

Rainy Days Can Be
Business Builders

SEASONAL

A rainy day is not a happy day for any salon. There's an old saying that goes, "If you've got lemons, make lemonade." As long as we're always going to have rainy days, let's try to make a little lemonade.

1 In winter and in other seasons, as well, clients will often come in with wet shoes. They've been trudging through slush in the parking lot, or a heavy rain has simply gotten their shoes and feet wet. Have a supply of paper slippers on hand. Give a pair of these to each wet-footed client, and then take her shoes over to the radiator. Her feet will be dry all during her salon services, and when she's ready to leave, her shoes will be dry, as well. So instead of discomfort and unhappiness throughout her salon visit, she'll be comfortable and appreciative. Comfortable and appreciative is much better for business than discomfort and unhappiness.

COMFORTABLE AND APPRECIATIVE IS MUCH BETTER FOR BUSINESS THAN IS COMFORT AND UNHAPPINESS.

2 How about the client who comes in without an umbrella but needs one by the time the salon visit is over? Even if she only has to run a short distance to her car in the parking lot, her hair will get wet, and we've got another unhappy situation. (Of course, you could give her the morning newspaper to hold over her head, but what do you do for the next client when there is no morning newspaper?)

Buy a dozen brightly colored umbrellas. Attach a luggage tag to each, identifying the umbrella as having come from your salon. Better yet, buy the umbrellas from a promotional supplies house that will imprint your salon's name and logo right on the umbrella. In an emergency rain situation, loan the umbrellas to clients who need them. They will absolutely bless you for your thoughtfulness and consideration.

If you're worried that you may lose too many umbrellas this way, don't be. People are decent. If they know that you've helped them out by loaning them an umbrella, they'll bring it back as soon as they can. And when they do bring it back, the chances are better than even that they'll be so appreciative of the help you gave them when they needed it that they'll book their next appointment there and then.

After you've done this awhile, you'll find that some salon clients and even former clients who get caught in the rain while shopping in the neighborhood—will stop in to ask if they can borrow an umbrella. Loan it to them graciously in the knowledge that their appreciation will result in nice talk, goodwill, and, inevitably, more business for your salon.

Put Spring to Work for You

SEASONAL

Spring, by and large, is a happy time. Clients are emerging from snow, sleet, and cold, trees are in bud, the birds are returning, and most people are in a happier frame of mind. You can accelerate this lovely feeling by making spring the star attraction during the month of March. Some suggestions:

1 Find yourself a friendly local florist. Ask him to fill your salon with flowers and plants—not just three pretty plants but lots of them—so that the moment a client opens the door, she'll know: Spring is here! Obviously, you don't want to *buy* all those plants. What would you do with them after the promotion was over? You want to try to "borrow" them for free during the promotional period.

What's in it for the florist? For one thing, he gets a sign in your salon that tells everyone that these gorgeous plants and flowers came from that wonderful florist. That's meaningful exposure to several hundred people, and he's bound to get some new customers out of this. Additionally, offer him, his wife, his staff free salon services during the promotional period. Obviously, you won't book these free services on busy days. Chances are that the florist's busy days are the same as yours, so he'll want to book the freebies during your slow periods, anyway.

2 The plants and flowers are just atmosphere to get people in the mood. By window signs, in-salon signs, postcards, local advertising, or flyers, let people know about the new spring hairstyles and/or services you're featuring in your salon.

Determine several styles and/or cuts that you want to feature, and make sure everyone on your staff can execute them. Feature highlighting, lightening soap caps, and the like. Spring conditioning is particularly appropriate after hair has been kept under hats or in heated rooms for several months.

YOU CAN ACCELERATE THIS LOVELY FEELING BY MAKING SPRING THE STAR ATTRACTION DURING THE MONTH OF MARCH.

3

If you really want to sweeten your whole spring promotional efforts, offer a small packet of seeds to everyone on your client mailing list. Send them each a postcard telling them about the plant and flower display, the spring styles and cuts, and services. And tell them you'll have a free packet of seeds waiting for them just for stopping in the salon. People can't resist seeds. They'll be certain to come by, and when they do, many of them will be happy and appreciative enough to book appointments before they leave the salon.

You know, of course, that it's difficult to get people to do what you want them to do (book an appointment) when they're in a bad mood. The opposite is also true. When they're in a good mood, when the surroundings are pleasant and fragrant, when they've just received a lovely and useful gift—you've got them.

Two Simple Salon Signs That Can Boost Your Spring Conditioning Business

Not all salon promotions need to involve elaborate preparation, details, mailings, advertisements, and the like. Some do, and that's fine, but some very simple things can qualify as "promotions" as well. The main thing is, always give your promotional ideas *thought* in terms of your own clientele, your own staff, your own capabilities. I once saw two simple signs in a salon that brought in a considerable amount of conditioning treatments, retail sales, and goodwill. The two signs were:

AN OUNCE OF

HAIR DAMAGE PREVENTION

IS WORTH A POUND OF

HAIR DAMAGE CURE.

AN OUNCE OF CONDITIONING

IS WORTH A POUND

OF RECONDITIONING.

There's basic, profound, and obvious wisdom in each of those signs. Clients reading them know immediately what the point is. But they're not so simple that you can just put up the two signs and expect a huge influx of business. No, you've got to give it more thought and preparation than that.

1 For starters, those signs should go up on the first day of spring. When people talk about spring, conversation and thought logically lead to summer. In this case, you don't want to wait until summer to talk about conditioning. Spring is your perfect lead-in.

2 The signs should be professionally done, not handmade with a felt-tipped pen. If you've got a computer and printer with a lot of fonts, you can turn out very respectable looking signs, especially if you've got a color printer. If you're not computerized, find a friend, relative, or client who is, and ask them to do it. Or make a deal with a professional sign painter and barter his services for yours.

TWO SIMPLE SIGNS CAN BRING IN A CONSIDERABLE AMOUNT OF CONDITIONING TREATMENTS, RETAIL SALES, AND GOODWILL.

3 Don't make just two signs. Make one sign for each styling station and shampoo station so that no matter what, every client will see the message.

4 Don't put up signs with Scotch tape. That's tacky and unprofessional. Frames are very reasonable nowadays; buy a supply of them and use them over and over as you try different promotional ideas.

5 Now you must have a staff meeting so that everyone knows the objectives of the season and the signs:

> Spring is here. It's nice to get outdoors and see the trees and leaves again, the flowers blooming, the grass growing, the temperatures comfortable. But soon enough temperatures will go into the 80s, 90s and higher, and people will be sunbathing and swimming and exposing their hair (and skin) to enormous potential damage. Everyone knows that sun bakes hair, water dries hair, salt water and chlorine are bad for hair. We expose our poor heads to all of this brutality, and the consequence is hair that is baked, cracked, split, and dried. You know it, your stylists know it, and indeed your clients know it. But they have to be *reminded* that all is not lost.

Clients need not wait for hair to be damaged for it to be rehabilitated. They can avoid damage by building up their hair in the weeks before and during the summer. How can they build hair up? Your two signs tell it all.

Prevention is the key. They can prevent hair damage by wearing hats or hairsprays with an SPF when they're in the sun, and they can condition their hair so that it can withstand the ravages of summer. During spring and summer, every salon visit should include suggestions for preventative conditioning treatments *and* suggestions for the purchase of proper shampoos and conditioners to use at home between salon visits.

6 Of course, you can do all of these suggestions without having those signs up in the salon. The purpose of the signs is to focus the client's attention on the idea of preventive conditioning—and to focus the attention of the stylists. Some clients may comment on the signs, and/or ask what they're all about, and, boom, the conversation is off and running. If the client doesn't comment, the stylist can very easily call their attention to the signs and what they mean.

After the signs have been up for a week or two, there will be some success stories where they resulted in treatments and retail sales. There'll also be some near misses and some strikeouts. That's the time to hold another staff meeting to discuss what worked for your people and what didn't. You'll learn what not to do because it didn't work and what to do because it did.

By the time the dog days of summer roll around, you'll find that you've done lots more conditioning business in the salon and have sold lots more conditioning products. You'll also get a wonderful intangible benefit: Your salon will be identified with good hair condition. Sadly, many clients can tell stories of hair damage in salons. On the other hand, *your* salon will be associated with great hair condition.

"The Danger Months"

Conversations between stylists and clients are sometimes trivial, sometimes gossipy, sometimes intimate, sometimes newsy. Usually a bare minimum of the conversations have to do with the subject of hair. Many stylists have trouble working the conversation around to hair, especially if the ultimate objective is to make some sort of retail sale. During June, July and August, it's very easy to help these stylists and increase their sale of retail hair care items. It's a fairly simple system:

MANY STYLISTS HAVE

TROUBLE WORKING

THE CONVERSATION

AROUND TO HAIR.

1 As with virtually all promotions, you've got to first sit down with all your stylists and explain what the promotion is all about, what it's intended to do, how everybody can go about doing it, and how everybody will benefit.

2 Buy a series of wall calendars. Prominently affix the months of June, July, and August in each styling station. Don't use Scotch tape. That looks tacky and cheap. Try rubber cement or any other adhesive that will do the job and be easily removed.

3 Using a paint brush and some red watercolor, paint an *X* through each of the months. An alternative would be to write THE DANGER MONTHS across the three months.

4 No client will be able to sit in any chair without asking, "What's all this about?" or "Are you guys closing for three months?" These questions or variations can propel the stylist right into a conversation about hair, and that's what we want.

5 Here's where the subject matter discussed in your staff meetings will be used to perfect advantage. We all know that many clients have lovely, well-conditioned hair on Memorial Day only to find that their hair is damaged, dry, and discolored when Labor Day rolls around. What has happened during those three "Danger Months" of June, July, and August? Very simple. Air, sun, heat, water, chlorine, salt water, neglect. Everyone knows about summer damage, but nobody does anything

about it. Why? Because they didn't get the appropriate advice from their stylists. They were talking about their kids or husbands or boyfriends or boss when they should have been talking about preventive measures during the Danger Months.

6 Advice is what every client needs. Product sales may come later, but advice is what they need first. They must be told about the destructive elements their hair will be exposed to during June, July, and August. They need some tips and pointers:

- Try to wear a bathing cap while swimming. If possible, rinse hair with clear water after exposure to chlorine or salt water. Few people wear bathing caps nowadays, but they should. If they do, some conditioner run through the hair before the cap goes on will help.

- Before sunbathing or exposure to water, saturate the hair with a conditioning oil or creme. If the client is going to sunbathe, at least let her hair be protected by conditioners during the process. Indeed, she'll actually be getting a hot-oil conditioning treatment.

- During exposure to the sun, suggest wearing a light-colored hat, cap, or turban. Of course, it will help if she applies a conditioning creme before the head covering goes on.

That's all great advice. And it's the kind of advice one friend would tell another, not a pushy sales talk. Be assured that when you give her the tip about applying a conditioning oil under a bathing cap or head covering when lying out in the sun, she will inevitably say something like, "Can you suggest one?" or "Is there a particular one you recommend?" The rest is easy.

7 While you're on the subject of summer, it is of course, good advice to tell her always to use a sunscreen as well as hair products with an appropriate SPF. (Do you stock several SPF numbers in spring and summer? If you don't, you should.)

It would help, too, and you would be doing your clients a favor, if you stocked some attractive bathing caps and head coverings. They'll buy them from you. The list can go on and on in terms of cremes, lotions, lip conditioners, sunscreen, makeup, and the like.

Remember, though, that you can stock all the appropriate items you want, but if your client walks right by them, ignores them, and nobody calls them to her attention, you'll have a lot of inventory left come Labor Day. But if every station has three calendar months with *X*s through them posted prominently, the conversation will be there, the attention will be paid, and the sales will be made.

IF EVERY STATION HAS THREE CALENDAR MONTHS WITH XS THROUGH THEM POSTED PROMINENTLY, THE CONVERSATION WILL BE THERE, THE ATTENTION WILL BE PAID, AND THE SALES WILL BE MADE.

Don't Let Summer
Be a Downer

SEASONAL

In many parts of the country spring signals pretty good business. People are coming out of winter, the leaves are on the trees, the flowers start to bloom, it's a time of renewal. "Renewal" doesn't just mean plants or trees; it affects humans, too, and that's why business increases during the spring months. But in many parts of the country, business dips significantly during the summer. Focus is outdoors rather than indoors; people take vacations and often work more on their tan than on their hair. Many salons accept this dip in business and sort of drift until fall. Don't be one of those salons! If traffic is decreased in July and August, you can make up for it by selling more retail products—and do your clients a favor at the same time.

At the tail end of spring, during May and June, when you think clients will be absent from the salon for extended periods of time. bring up the subject of summer so that you can counsel clients on what to do during those months to maintain their hair condition. Remind them that hair care is a year-round proposition. If they're going to be away from the salon for an extended period, make sure they take with them the professional hair care products they need. Here are some:

Shampoo. Yes, your clients have a supply of shampoo in their bathrooms, but during the summer they'll be going to the beach and swimming pools. They'll need an extra bottle or tube of shampoo to take along with them to get the salt water or chlorine out of their hair.

Conditioners. Same as shampoos. Your clients have them at home, but they ought to have an extra one in a little kit or bag to take with them on all outdoor outings.

Moisturizing Lotions. The sun dries out skin, and your clients know it. Your recommendation of an appropriate product will be appreciated.

Lip Conditioners. Do you carry them? If not, you should. They're needed in summer to keep lips from becoming parched.

Suntan Lotions.   Many salons don't carry these, but you should, if only in summer. It is an established fact that these creams, liquids, and lotions with the appropriate SPF number prevent the burn but not the tan.

Blow-dryer, Nail Polish, Cosmetics.   Yes, your client has all of these, but does she have them for her locker at the golf course or swimming pool?

The point of all this is that these summer needs are very realistic. Just because you and your staff don't talk about them doesn't mean the need will go away. They'll be discovered by clients in emergency situations. They'll be outdoors somewhere, or on vacation, and realized that they don't have one, two, or even all, of these products. They don't panic, however; they simply go into the local drugstore or supermarket and buy all the products they need—products they would have bought from you had you reminded them.

This is not pushy or high-pressure selling. It is conversational, friendly, advisory selling. Bring it all up during casual conversation with the client. If you haven't managed to do it by the time she's ready to get out of the chair, at least do it then in the form of a checklist:

> You're going to be spending a lot of time in the sun in the next few weeks. A lot of our clients pack a special bag to always carry with them whenever they go to a pool or the beach or any other outdoor activity. I like to remind clients, so they won't be stuck anywhere without the things they need in a travel supply. So will you be needing an extra travel supply of shampoo, conditioner, moisturizer, lip conditioner, suntan lotion, nail polish, cosmetics, or a hairbrush or blow-dryer?

Changes are at least one and probably more will hit the mark, and you'll make a sale.

This is an activity everyone in the salon should practice on every client they work on all during May, June, July, and August. If every stylist at least goes through the checklist with every client, retail sales will significantly increase. This may not totally make up for the dip in summer business, but it will partially do the trick, and you'll at least be attacking the problem instead of lamenting it.

THIS IS NOT PUSHY OR HIGH-PRESSURE SELLING. IT IS CONVERSATIONAL, FRIENDLY, ADVISORY SELLING.

Promo 8 | "Show and Tell" Mailing Gets Business Going

SEASONAL

PRINTED MATERIAL

GET IN ON THE

"SHOW AND TELL"

ACT BY SHARING YOUR

EXPERIENCES WITH

YOUR CLIENTELE.

The whole "Show and Tell" phenomenon is a permanent part of our culture. After kids go back to school, they come home on the very first day to say that they had Show and Tell. It's fun, and they get to share their summer experiences with each other. You can get in on the act by sharing your experiences—more accurately, your whole crew's experiences—with your clientele. But with a difference. You want to Show and Tell not what you all did on vacation but how you all spent your time productively elevating your professional skills. Here's how to do it.

1. Schedule a salon meeting with your entire staff sometime early in May. Explain to them the importance of continuing their education and upgrading their skill levels in all aspects of cosmetology and related fields. Explain that in the fall you'll be promoting their individual talents, individual areas of expertise, and individual efforts at upgrading professional skills. Encourage them, without pressure, to take courses, attend classes, participate in workshops, and attend shows in any areas of the profession that interest them. Get as many people as possible involved in as many classes as possible during June, July, and August.

2. As various members of the staff complete their classes, keep accurate records of who took what class in what area. As August draws to a close you're ready to start gearing up for your Show and Tell activity.

3. Notify all of your clients about what you've all been doing. Prepare a mailing something like this:

SHOW AND TELL

Here's What We've Been Doing All Summer

At Betty's Beauty Nook we consider it to be not only our job but our *responsibility* to stay absolutely current with new trends, products, techniques, and hair fashions so that we can assure you that you're getting not only the best but also the very latest in all aspects of beauty.
So here's what we've been up to:

Betty Jones attended classes on hairstyling with So-and-So at the Such-and-Such Beauty Show in This-and-This city.

Mary Smith attended a Workshop on Braiding, given by industry expert So-and-So.

Gloria Brown, Debra Abbott, and Fran Bennett all attended the International Haircolor Exchange in Memphis, Tennessee, where they took part in lectures and workshops with ten of the top haircolorist/teachers in the USA.

Helen Dunn took classes in nail art with So-and-so, one of the industry's top experts, in This-and-This city.

[You can see the way you should structure this. Mention every bit of learning that every member of the staff acquired during the summer months. Tell who the teacher was. Indicate the city so that they know you're all ranging far and wide in the pursuit of knowledge.]

As always we will be delighted to see you so that we can show you the new knowledge we've gained, the new products we've discovered.

Call for an appointment today. We're looking forward to seeing you.
BETTY'S BEAUTY NOOK • 622 Oak Street • New City • Tel. 789-2345

This mailing to all of your clients will motivate people to call for appointments. If you want to attract people who aren't currently clients— and why wouldn't you?—put up a big sign in your window. You don't have to state all the details, just the essentials: who took what course in what subject plus a restatement of your salon's dedication to always expose clients to the very latest and the very best.

Even if you don't put a sign in the window to attract new clients, here's what your mailing to existing clients will do:

- It will assure them that you're keeping up with the very latest—and you may be assured that this will impress them.
- September is a busy time, and many clients may not have beauty appointments on their minds. This will remind them that the beauty "season" has started.
- The word-of-mouth can be considerable. At meetings, get-togethers, social conversions, there will be occasions when someone will say with some pride, "My salon really keeps up with the latest. . . ."
- You will just *naturally* do more business because of all the new skills your staff has acquired. Education does pay off. The more competent everybody becomes, the better work they'll do, the more satisfied the customers will be, the greater the reputation of the salon will be.

EDUCATION IS

A NEVER-ENDING,

NONSEASONAL

ENDEAVOR.

All of this doesn't mean that everyone's educational activities should only be confined to the summer months. Far from it. Education is a never-ending, nonseasonal endeavor. The purpose of this promotion is very simply and purely to get the work out and to get in step with the Show and Tell season while everybody else is marching to that same drummer.

Capitalize on Sun Damage

SEASONAL

PRINTED MATERIAL

When summer is over, just about every woman in America has to live with one of its legacies—damaged hair. Summer is a time of exposure to the sun (damage), salt water (damage), chlorine (damage), wet combing and brushing (damage). You almost don't have to point it out to them. They know it, but they may not think of doing anything about it professionally. Many will just think, "I'll just glop some more conditioner on when I shampoo." What you want to do is "Ask for the order." Tell them they've got a problem, and you've got the solution. Some ways to do it are:

1 Postcards that say:

> IS YOUR HAIR IN WORSE CONDITION IN SEPTEMBER
> THAN IT WAS IN MAY? YOU BET IT IS!

Let us nurse it back to health. We are hair reconditioning *experts*.

After a summer of heat, sun, salt water, chlorine, and wet combing and brushing, your hair has to be suffering. We can eliminate the pain with deep-conditioning treatments, easy-to-care-for cuts, professional at-home products, and expert advice on how to make your hair happy again.

Come in for a free, no-obligation analysis and consultation.

2 The postcards will ring a bell with those who are conscious of their damaged hair, but it will do more. Many women somehow seem to put their salon appointments on hold during the summer months. They'll get around to coming in again as fall sets in and the holiday season approaches. But your postcard mailed right around Labor Day will be a reminder. So instead of waiting until October, clients may be motivated to book their appointment in early September.

3 Your promotion doesn't have to begin and end with mailing out postcards. You can certainly put a sign in your window saying:

IS YOUR HAIR IN WORSE CONDITION IN SEPTEMBER
THAN IT WAS IN MAY? YOU BET IT IS!

Let us nurse it back to health.
We are hair reconditioning experts.

A window sign will bring in a certain number of people who are not now your salon's clients, and that's a plus. Too many windows are underutilized. You've got a lot of square footage display space available to you, and you should always put part of it to work for you via signs.

4 During the whole month of September, make it a point to counsel clients on how to keep their hair in optimum condition. Don't make it an obvious pitch for selling them a retail product or a salon treatment. Just give them honest and sincere advice. Tell them how to towel dry their hair, how to comb or brush it while wet, how to use conditioners at home, even if they are grocery-store conditioners.

5 When the conversation is easy, unpushy, helpful, and sincere, clients will relax and start asking questions. When they do, you'll have the opportunity to explain the need for professional as well as at-home treatments, the superiority of the conditioning treatments and products you carry, and so on. Once you're having a conversation on hair conditioning, it's almost inevitable that you'll sell either an in-salon treatment, an at-home treatment, or both.

Keep in mind that this kind of conversation, even if it doesn't result in a sale, is certainly preferable to a discussion about her personal problems—or yours. The most important asset you have is your knowledge and expertise. When you talk about hair, you're using this asset. When you talk about personal stuff, you're keeping your most valuable asset in the closet. Let it out, and September is one of the best months to do it.

First-Aid Station for Damaged Hair

Very often business drops off during the summer. People are away on vacation, they're more informal, they may not keep up their schedule of salon visits. But they'll be back again after Labor Day. The kids are off to school, the social season is warming up, and they see that their hair has been damaged by wind, water, chlorine, sun, salt water, and neglect. Your steady clients will drift back and will be open to suggestions for hair and hair color reconditioning, rehabilitation, and refreshment. If you're located on street level, hundreds and hundreds of women pass your salon who are *not* your clients, but you may be assured that their hair has been just as ravaged by the summer—maybe even more so. Perhaps they'll be planning visits to their regular salons and perhaps not, but it can only help if you reach out to them. Here's how.

SEASONAL

PRINTED MATERIAL

1 Have a big white sign made up that fills at least half of your window. Have a big red cross painted on the sign and, in big black letters, say something like:

> FIRST-AID STATION FOR DAMAGED HAIR.
>> SUN DAMAGE . . .
>> WIND DAMAGE . . .
>> SALTWATER DAMAGE . . .
>> BLEACH DAMAGE . . .
>
> . . . CAN ALL BE REMEDIED.
>> FREE CONSULTATION
>> NO APPOINTMENT
>> NO OBLIGATION

Just bring your damaged hair inside.

Will people, including your clients, notice? Without a doubt. Will it bring in some new clients as well as old ones? Positively.

HUNDREDS OF WOMEN PASS YOUR SALON WHO ARE NOT CLIENTS, BUT THEIR HAIR HAS BEEN JUST AS RAVAGED BY THE SUMMER—MAYBE MORE SO.

NOTES

Two or three of your staff who are particularly gifted in communication skills should be assigned the task of doing the consultations.

Try to take the people who walk in for the free consultations as quickly as possible. If they can't be seen immediately, tell them it will be five, ten, or fifteen minutes. If you can't see them within fifteen minutes, schedule an actual appointment time for the free consultation. A tremendous amount of goodwill is involved here, and you don't want to blow it by inviting people in and not delivering.

The consultation should be honest and detailed. It won't be hard. The consultant will very easily be able to see what's wrong, why it happened, and what can be done about it. Do it all in a straightforward manner. Never insult the client or her hairdresser. (*No* "How could you let this happen?" or "Who did this to you?")

As you make suggestions for home remedies, find out what products they generally use at home. Don't insult those, either. You can simply tell them that you're not familiar with every product on the market, but you are completely familiar with the product(s) you use, recommend, and prescribe. Don't use pressure. It will be resented, and you'll lose the precious opportunity to build goodwill. They'll be happy with the advice. They'll be grateful, and chances are they'll buy the product(s) you prescribe. If they don't, that's fine, too. Remember, you promised: No obligation.

Where color is concerned, you can be a little more forceful. Chances are that even if a person is given the best possible advice by a truly competent haircolorist, she won't be able to adequately make the color and conditioning corrections herself. If she wants the advice, give it to her, but let her know she is in technical deep water, and she would be best advised to have her color corrected by a professional.

Leave the sign in the window for the entire month of September. By the time you take it down, you will have made many new friends, all of them potential clients and a good percentage of them now actual clients. Success!

Cut and Condition Promotion a Natural for September

SEASONAL

When Labor Day comes and summer draws to a close, most women are aware that something has to be done with their hair. They have been out-doors, they haven't paid the attention they should to their hair's condition, they haven't had as many occasions to style it and have it look its best. The sun may have bleached out some of the color and, surely, a great deal of the moisture. But knowing that something has to be done and actually doing it are two different things. People get involved in back-to-school and other post-Labor Day activities and delay doing that "something" about their hair. It's up to you to remind them.

1 In this particular case, I'd suggest a personal letter. Sure, people get a lot of junk mail and throw away a lot of it without even looking at it. But a letter from their favorite beauty salon won't be categorized as "junk." They know you, you have a relationship. They're bound to want to know what it is you want to say to them. So a letter will be a particularly good device.

2 You've got to compose the letter thoughtfully. It can't be a "canned" message that doesn't sound as though it's coming from your brain and your heart. Of course, you'll tell them that you hope they've had a nice summer. But you'll also go on to explain that summer sun and its activities in wind, chlorine, and salt water do monstrous damage to hair. Some of the damage is reversible with deep-conditioning salon treatments and professional home preparations. But some of the damage can be so irreversible as to require cutting it off. What could be more appropriate than a brand-new fall haircut that gets rid of the damaged ends and styles the hair for the coming months? That fall haircut, combined with the needed conditioning, is what you want to make available to them.

3 Your promotion should give them a conditioning treatment *free* when they book a haircut appointment.

4 Put a time limit on this offer. The time limit can be either that they must come in for their appointment by October 1st, or they must call by October 1st to book the appointment for whatever date they'd like.

THE POINT OF YOUR
LETTER WILL BE FOR
THEM TO THINK,
"YES, SHE'S RIGHT.
I'M GOING TO GIVE
THEM A CALL."

The point of your letter will be for them to think, "Yes, she's right. My hair does look dried out and washed out, and I haven't had a haircut since May. My hair can use a good conditioning treatment, too. I'm going to give them a call."

5 When your client comes in for that cut and condition, the conditioning treatment you use should be the one you want to sell her when she walks out the door. Include a few minutes of scalp massage in your treatment. Tell her exactly what product you're using and *why* you are using it. You've got half a dozen conditioning products for sale in your salon, and she'll see a dozen more when she does her shopping. She has to know— you've got to tell her—why this particular conditioner was selected by you to use on her in the salon and is recommended for use at home.

6 Make certain that she sees a tube or jar of this specific product before you actually use it on her. Leave a retail package of the product right there on the station counter as you style and cut her hair. When it's all done, and her hair looks a thousand percent better than it did when she walked in, simply ask her if she'd like to have this product for use at home. She'll take it. Why wouldn't she? You've given it your endorsement and recommendation. You've used it and the results are beautiful.

7 This entire promotion actually takes relatively little time and money between postage and printing. You can send out a few hundred letters for $100 to $200. The first few haircuts will pay for that expenditure. All the rest is gravy.

Remember that if you get women coming in to get their hair cut in September, they'll surely want it cut again before Thanksgiving. If you don't remind them, and they don't have their after-summer cut until late October-early November, you won't be cutting them for Thanksgiving. So this promotion actually can push hundreds, or thousands, of additional dollars into your till—to say nothing of all the extra retail conditioners you're going to sell. Write those letters!

Your Hair Is Either
Dying of Thirst or Freezing

Winter is not an especially good time for hair. Hair dries out when it's indoors, and it's exposed to cold shock when it's outdoors. Also, hair is often covered with hats, scarves, and hoods, which mat it down and keep the scalp from breathing. Whenever we observe a negative influence on hair, we can turn it into a positive occurrence in the salon.

SEASONAL

This particular campaign lends itself to postcards. You can have some printed up in a certain font, or you can write the message out and have your printer reproduce your handwriting as a more personalized message. The postcards go to all clients and former clients who haven't been in the salon for a couple of months. They can also go to nonclients if you get appropriate community mailing lists, women's club memberships, and new residents. You'd be amazed at how selective mailing lists can be nowadays. You can often pinpoint not only the neighborhoods you'd like to cover but also the kinds of clients you'd like to attract: young or old, married or single, certain income levels, and so forth. The Yellow Pages usually have listings under the heading Mailing Lists. If you come from a particularly small town and your phone book doesn't have this listing, go to the phone directory of the next biggest town.

PRINTED MATERIAL

WHENEVER WE OBSERVE A NEGATIVE INFLUENCE ON HAIR, WE CAN TURN IT INTO A POSITIVE OCCURRENCE IN THE SALON.

Your message is a simple one:

YOUR HAIR IS EITHER DYING OF THIRST OR FREEZING.

Do you know what winter does to your hair? Indoors, heated temperatures pull the moisture out. Outdoors, freezing temperatures create shock and havoc. If you try to protect your hair by covering it with a hat, hood, scarf, or whatnot, you smother your scalp.

What's the solution? Scalp and hair massage, cleansing and moisturizing. Experience it yourself. Even one treatment can do wonders. Do your hair a favor. Call for an appointment.

People who call for an appointment will generally fall into one of two categories.

1 The terminal-damage type. This will be a client whose hair was damaged long before winter. She's unhappy with it, doesn't know what to do about it, and finally simply accepts it. When your card comes in, there is hope. You say that one treatment can make a difference. She decides to call.

2 The "I care about my hair" type. This person may not have much damage, but she knows that the message in your card makes sense. She wants to head off trouble before it starts. She can be one of the most valuable clients of all because she values her hair so highly.

Remember, when clients call for their appointments and/or come in, they're interested in hair conditioning rather than color or style. Analyze the hair, and give it the best kind of treatment you know how to give. A ten to fifteen minute scalp massage to begin with will relax the client and make her happy that she came.

Shampoo the client's hair with the mildest shampoo you have. Tell her what you're doing and explain why. (Be assured she'll buy that shampoo on the way out.)

Now comes the conditioning treatment. Remember, the client or potential client who really cares about her hair can be a source of income for years to come. Don't do any kind of quickie job on her. Use a heavy-duty conditioner. It's often a good idea to use a thick oil or cream and to wrap her hair turban style in a damp, warm level. She'll love that.

SOMETIMES A HAIRCUT

IS THE ONLY SOLUTION.

NOW YOU'VE GOT

A CUTTING CLIENT

IN ADDITION TO A

CONDITIONING CLIENT.

There may be damaged ends that are beyond redemption. You'll have to explain how they got that way. If hair is chin to shoulder length, those ends are a year or two old. That's alot of exposure to sun and wind, hundreds of showers, countless hours of blowing. If she's administered her own perming or haircoloring, that surely will have contributed. Explain that hair is not a living organism. With your expertise and products at your disposal, you can make it look better, feel better, act better. You can keep it in great condition, but sometimes those ends have been subjected to so much protracted abuse that a haircut is the only solution. Now you've got a cutting client in addition to a conditioning client.

Suggest products for the client to use at home. Tell her how to use them. Suggest that she massage her own scalp several times a week. Suggest that she buy a humidifier to put moisture into the air of her dry, heated home. Will she see a difference in even one treatment? Of course she will. You know that. But that shouldn't stop you from suggesting that during the winter months it is a very good idea to come in once a month for a full professional salon-conditioning treatment. Get her to realize that prevention of damage is far preferable to treating damage. Make her an offer she can't refuse. If she comes in for three full-conditioning sessions, the fourth is free. By the time she finishes that fourth treatment, she'll be hooked. And all this came about because of a postcard solicitation.

How to Increase Business When It Snows

SEASONAL

PRINTED MATERIAL

DISCOUNT OFFER

TELL CLIENTS AND

POTENTIAL CLIENTS

THAT ON ANY DAY

THAT THERE IS SNOW,

THEY CAN CALL FOR

APPOINTMENTS ON

THAT DAY AND RECEIVE

A DISCOUNT.

In a good part of the country snow is not a problem. The climate is such that snowflakes are never seen. But in a larger percentage of our country, snow presents a particular problem for salon owners: cancellations. Clients see a few flurries and think they ought to cancel their hair appointment. This can, of course, be devastating to business—unless you do something about it. Try a "Snow Check." It's a first cousin to the rain checks used at athletic events and many retail establishments. It's very simple:

1 Design your Snow Check so that it is the size of a postcard. Tell clients and potential clients that on any day that there is snow, they can call for appointments on that day and receive a discount.

2 Obviously, how much of a discount is up to you. If snow cancellations are a major problem, you ought to make the discount generous, 25 percent or more. If snow cancellations are a relatively minor problem, you can offer a 10 percent or 15 percent discount.

3 Send these Snow Checks out to every client on your address list. If you'd like, expand it to a more general mailing list, including nonclients. Tell them to save the card and present it when they come for their appointment to receive the discount. When they come in for their discounted snow check services, you can issue them yet another one for next time it snows.

4 You'll find that some people will actually wait for a snow day to call in for an appointment. Nothing wrong with that. It may impel them to make an appointment a few weeks before they might normally do so.

5 Then there's the matter of what happens if it's a severe winter, and there are a lot of snow days. Nothing so terrible about that. If it snows a lot and people use their Snow Checks a lot, it means that in a severe winter your salon is crowded with people while other salons are crying the blues because of cancellations.

6 If you live in a snowy area, you may even want to take out a small ad in a very local publication (Pennysavers, for example) and have a Snow Check coupon. That won't cost you very much, but it will expose your Snow Check promotion to a number of people who aren't regular clients. Every time somebody clips this coupon and brings it in on a snow day, it means you have attracted a new client. If they're pleased with their service, you've got them for the rest of the year at regular prices.

7 Don't be too fussy about "measurable" snow. If you insist that it be at least a half-inch or one-inch or two-inch snowfall, you'll come to grief debating with clients whether any particular snow qualifies for use of the Snow Check. You can't win that kind of debate. If a client calls and says, "It's snowing in my neighborhood, can I come in?" tell her, "Sure." The whole idea is to keep traffic coming into your salon during inclement weather, to attract some new clients, and to have some fun. Snow Checks will do it all.

Holidays &
Events

A New Year's Resolution Will
Bring in Customers

HOLIDAY

The fall-early winter season is, thank Heaven, a busy time in most salons. Back to school, changing wardrobes, changing looks, Thanksgiving, Christmas, and New Year's. A wonderful, busy time—and then it abruptly drops off dramatically. Because usually takes a pretty good rest in January/February, but it need not be so. All too often salons and stylists pause for a little rest themselves right after the first of the year.

There's a saying that professional salespeople live by: "You've got to ask for the order." In other words, it's not just enough to make a good sales presentation. You've got to end by actually asking for the order. Otherwise it all just drifts off into conversation. Your salon, too, must "Ask for the order," especially right after Christmas/New Year's.

There are all kinds of ways to do this. They are enumerated all over the pages of this book, but one that plays right into this specific holiday season is to make a *public* New Year's resolution. Everybody's making resolutions at this time; newspapers are full of them, conversations are full of them. Get in on it. Have a big sign made for your window that says:

YOUR SALON, TOO, MUST "ASK FOR THE ORDER," ESPECIALLY RIGHT AFTER CHRISTMAS/ NEW YEAR'S.

OUR RESOLUTION FOR THE NEW YEAR:
TO KEEP YOUR HAIR IN PERFECT CONDITION.
Come in. Let's talk.

Put that sign up in the window right after Christmas, and keep it up during the entire month of January. That's it, just a sign. Here's what it can accomplish:

1 Existing clients coming in for regular appointments may say, "I want to make the same resolution. How are we going to do it?" That gives you the chance to talk about the appropriate cut, color, perm, in-salon conditioning, home maintenance of the style, at-home conditioning, and retail sales.

2 It may push the "hot button" of nonclients passing by. A great percentage of the population has hair-conditioning problems. They live with them, they adapt to them, they get to be philosophical about

them—but they don't like them. The sign is translated in their minds to say, "There is hope." The gentle invitation "Come in. Let's talk" may be just enough to get them to cross your threshold. Then it's up to you. Once the conditioning conversation gets started, don't let it continue with the client, or potential client, standing up. You want to sit her down. That will keep her from shifting from one leg to the other and maybe making a too-hasty departure.

3 Do an honest and sincere "intake" of the clients' problems, habits, lifestyle, and the products she uses. Comb through her hair, touch it, feel it, get a sense of it yourself. You're a professional, and it won't be difficult for you to make a diagnosis.

4 Patiently explain to the client exactly what her problem is and what she should do about it. Don't be overbearing, don't be critical, don't knock her previous hairdresser. Just talk to her as one friend would to another.

5 Obviously your "prescription" will include salon visits and the purchase and use of some of the products you sell. Make sure to include other ingredients like instruction on how she should treat her hair and use the appropriate products. Products alone don't do the job. They must be properly used.

6 Give her the assurance and reassurance of your "guarantee." Assure her that if she follows your advice to the letter, she *will* have excellent hair condition, and you will see to it that it always stays that way. Is that too much to "guarantee?" Not at all; it's the truth. If she becomes a client and follows your program of salon and home maintenance, why wouldn't she have great hair condition?

Then there's the instance of the nonclient who just comes in for some advice and counseling. Give it to her fully. Don't give her short shrift. She may simply be testing you to see if you're going to be pushy, overbearing, or pressure her. When you are your honest, sincere, soft-sell self, she's a better-than-even possibility of becoming a client in the future.

And remember, all of this is a heck of a lot better than sitting around in January, lamenting about how slow business is.

Valentine's Day Is the Perfect Time to Sell Gift Certificates

HOLIDAY

PRINTED MATERIAL

Valentine's Day is the perfect time to sell gift certificates to men *and* women. You'll be aided by lots of newspaper, television, and magazine advertising by retailers. Nowadays everyone knows that Valentine's Day is a "holiday" and that it's appropriate, and in some cases obligatory, to buy a gift for one's Valentine.

Studies have shown that more men buy Valentine gifts for women than vice versa. It's also an observed habit that the guys think about buying a Valentine's Day gift at the last minute, and they simply don't know what to get. Help them along.

Put a big sign in your window advertising that you have gift certificates available. The message can be stated in any one of several ways . . .

HOW MUCH DO YOU REALLY LOVE HER?
GIVE HER A BEAUTY GIFT CERTIFICATE.

OR

THE PERFECT VALENTINE'S DAY GIFT.
A GIFT CERTIFICATE FOR A DAY OF BEAUTY.

OR

SHOW HER YOU LOVE HER.
A BEAUTY GIFT CERTIFICATE
IS THE PERFECT VALENTINE'S GIFT.

> IT'S APPROPRIATE, AND IN SOME CASES OBLIGATORY, TO BUY A GIFT FOR ONE'S VALENTINE.

You must, of course, have gift certificates printed up. The classic kind would have a sort of filigree border. The copy would read: "This Certificate entitles _____ to $_____ dollars of beauty services." That wording covers certificates for any amount the person would want to spend.

Many salons, however, are getting away from certificates that define a specific dollar amount. They have found that some people shy away from a gift that tells the recipient how much they spent, thinking it's tacky. Instead, you can have a *series* of gift certificates made up that would enumerate the specific services that the certificate is for. Figure out different packages of services. Then you can sell some certificates for $25, some for $50, $75, $100, or more. Your top-price certificate should be for "The Works" or "A Day of Beauty." These would include a variety of hair services, manicure and pedicure services, and perhaps skin care services.

Throw in an escalating scale of bonuses that would be included. The bigger the gift certificate amount, the bigger the bonus. Bonuses can include services, or, more likely, retail products. So when someone buys a certificate and it is redeemed, you not only perform the service on either new or existing clients, but you also get them started on one or more retail products.

It's a winner all the way. The man is off the hook, the woman is delighted and you've got money in the till.

There is somewhat of a variation on this promotion. Many women are unhappy with their husband's haircut or hairstyle. This is especially so among salon clients. They've been exposed to good styling in the salon, and they know that their husband or boyfriend just goes to Joe the barber. I know a salon that printed this copy:

VALENTINE'S DAY GIFT CERTIFICATE . . .
for one of the best haircuts you've ever had

When the men come in to redeem their certificates, you have a whole new group of potential clients. Once men feel a little bit at home in the salon atmosphere and realize the extra attention, styling alternatives, and professional competence of stylists, they very often become hooked.

The two- or three-week period before Valentine's Day is kind of a "love season." Allowing people to express their love by fattening your gross is simply a delicious idea. Go for it!

The Perfect Gift for
Mother's Day

HOLIDAY

PRINTED MATERIAL

Next to Christmas, Mother's Day gets more promotional hype and hoopla than any other holiday. Starting two to four weeks before Mother's Day virtually every retail establishment is beating the drums for Mother's Day business. All of this activity starts husbands, sons, and daughters down the anguished annual path of "What can I get her *this* year." It's a dilemma everyone has faced and will continue to face. And since everyone is pondering this problem, why not provide them with a solution—a Mother's Day gift certificate. It's perfect! As soon as people know about it, they'll breathe a sigh of relief: Problem solved. Let's do it!

1 If your salon is in a strip mall, or any other street-level location where there is plenty of traffic, a big sign in the window will do the trick. It can say simply:

> We have the perfect gift for Mother's Day
> and we GUARANTEE she'll love it!
> Information inside.

2 If you're not in a high traffic area but know a few spots where flyers can be distributed, print some up saying:

> We have the perfect gift for Mother's Day
> and we GUARANTEE she'll love it . . .
> A gift certificate at the Color & Comb Salon.
> Your gift can be for any amount or any service you choose.
> Shampoo, Cut, Restyle, Blowout, Color, Perm, Facial, Manicure.

WHAT COULD BE BETTER FOR MOM THAN THE GIFT OF BEAUTY AND
PAMPERING.

Color and Comb Salon • 1234 Broadway • Riverside • Tel. 987-6543

Give these away by the hundreds. Chances are, the sale of your first gift certificate will pay for the whole printing job.

NEXT TO CHRISTMAS,
MOTHER'S DAY GETS
MORE PROMOTIONAL
HYPE AND HOOPLA
THAN ANY OTHER
HOLIDAY.

THE TIDE OF

HAPPINESS ON

MOTHER'S DAY

WASHES UNTOLD

MILLIONS INTO

BUSINESSES. YOU'RE

ONE OF THESE

BUSINESSES.

3 Make sure you get the name, address, and family relationship of everyone who buys a gift certificate. Put them on a mailing list for next year, and every year thereafter, and most of them will want to repeat! It's such an easy solution to the "What should I get" problem that people will be happy you're providing them with a solution year after year.

4 Pay special and particular attention to the women who bring in the gift certificates for redemption. Each one has to love the experience and be so happy when she leaves that she calls her husband, son, or daughter with special expressions of appreciation. The givers will remember how much Mom enjoyed the experience when you solicit them again the following year. Over time, your mailing list of potential Mother's Day gift certificate givers will be substantial. This promotion alone will make May into one of your best months of the year.

All your clients should associate their salon experiences with happiness. Certain times of the year are, in general, associated with happiness. Mother's Day is one of them. Don't let this period go by as just another couple of weeks in the working year. The tide of happiness on Mother's Day washes untold millions into businesses. You're one of these businesses. Grab some of that happiness for yourself.

The Unisex concept has been a blessing for beauty salons. It has brought millions of men into salons who, in the past, simply had their hair cut at barbershops. The fact remains, however, that in most salons, the percentage of male clientele is quite small. It's all very nice business. It's business we wouldn't have if they were still going to barbershops, but in most salons you seldom see men. Attracting more men is one way to profit by male business. Another is to get them to spend more when they do come to the salon. It's the latter consideration that this particular Father's Day promotion is beamed at.

OK, say you have men who patronize your salon. They may be a few, they may be many, but they probably share one characteristic: They come only to have their hair cut. They rarely avail themselves of other services in the salon the way women do. Our job is to craft a promotion that will get them to expand their vistas by exposing them to some of the other jobs of the salon experience.

1 This promotion is going to be giving away services. You shouldn't think that this will either cheat your salon or dilute your earnings. Quite the contrary. We're going to be "sampling" salon services to male clients who are fathers. There are clients who would be content to come in every month or so, forever, and just sit down, have their hair cut, and walk out the door. Female clients, on the other hand, avail themselves of a host of services other than haircutting. So, for one short period we are going to be very generous with men. If we succeed, and we certainly will in a percentage of cases, we'll be getting significantly more revenue from male clients than had been the case. In this promotion we'll offer male clients who are fathers any additional salon service they choose at absolutely no charge when they come in during this particular month to have their hair cut. "That's right, Mr. Jones, when you schedule an appointment to have your hair cut, you can also have a manicure or a facial treatment or a therapeutic scalp massage or even a perm or coloring."

GET MEN TO EXPAND THEIR VISTAS BY EXPOSING THEM TO OTHER JOYS OF THE SALON EXPERIENCE.

The men will be overjoyed. It will be very rare that a man will choose a perm or coloring, so most of the services will add only fifteen to twenty minutes to his regular appointment time. Even if a man chooses to have his hair colored, wouldn't that be great? Now every month that he comes in for a cut, he'll also schedule a retouch. He becomes just about twice as profitable as before. So relax, look ahead, and accept this basic premise of the additional free service.

2 On the Monday morning immediately after Mother's Day, put up a sign in your window and in a prominent place in your salon saying:

ATTENTION FATHERS

We're celebrating FATHER'S DAY during the entire month of June by giving away FREE SALON SERVICES to all fathers when they get their hair cut!

Fathers, when you schedule your appointment you have your choice of any of the following FREE: Manicure, Mini-Facial, Fifteen-Minute Therapeutic Scalp Massage, Perm, Hair Color, Highlighting, Deep Conditioning.

Schedule your appointment now!

HAPPY FATHER'S DAY!

3 What happens when you have a young client in his 20s or 30s who isn't a father, and he says "Hey, how about me?" Have fun with it and say, "Well, someday you'll be a father, right?" and give him the service he requests. After all, you're expanding your base of business.

4 Have each of your fathers "register" by giving you his name and address, his spouse's name, and the names of each of his children. Put this information on file. During the course of the year, you may want to have another promotion uniquely suited to men. These names will be your basic mailing list. People who participate in one promotion will usually participate in another. So this idea can actually perpetuate itself.

MEN CARE ABOUT THEIR APPEARANCE EVERY BIT AS MUCH AS WOMEN.

Keep in mind that wanting variety is a human characteristics, one not confined to females. Men care about their appearance every bit as much as women. They want to look good to their peers, to the opposite sex, to their co-workers, and they want to give themselves rewards now and then.

In the old barbershop days men would get a shave in the barbershop even though they could certainly shave themselves. They loved the experience of the hot towel and the splash of aftershave when it was over. The same impulse that motivated men then will be at work here when they treat themselves to the various salon services you're offering. Suddenly they'll stop being sheepish about booking themselves for a manicure. Some will sign on for the ultimate pampering, a facial treatment. And you can absolutely count on more men starting to color their hair as a result of the "encouragement" you give them by doing it free with this Father's Day Special.

On Election Day You're
Always on the Winning Side

HOLIDAY

It's always impressive when you know that a certain salon has celebrities as part of it's clientele. And, of course, whoever is the hairdresser to the First Lady inevitably gets national coverage in magazines. Naturally, most salons don't have national celebrities living in or visiting their community, but everyone has local celebrities. Who are they? The politicians—or their spouses.

During any given election year there are usually a handful of people running for office in your immediate locality. Depending on the size of your town or city, people running for mayor, councilman, alderman, supervisor, legislator, and so on may be living somewhere nearby. Their pictures are in the papers during election season. People know their names. They are local celebrities. Let's get these local celebrities into your salon.

1 Wouldn't it be a nice touch for you to invite the spouses of local candidates and local candidates themselves into your salon for free salon services during the two weeks immediately preceding Election Day?

2 Chances are you can find everyone's address in the telephone directory. If they're unlisted, write to them care of their local campaign headquarters. Make sure the envelope reads PRIVATE & CONFIDENTIAL. TO BE OPENED ONLY BY [NAME OF PERSON]. Tell them you know how harried their schedules must be. Tell them you're willing to shift your schedule around on short notice to accommodate them. And tell them that the services they receive will be with your compliments.

3 How can all of this activity benefit your salon? First, contact your local newspaper and tell them what you're doing. Tell them it's your way of showing your appreciation to people who are dedicating themselves to public service. It's an interesting, out-of-the-ordinary slant on election news, and the beauty editor, or even the news editor, may think it's just cute enough to give it coverage. If they do, that's great publicity for your salon. But even if they don't, there are major benefits to be derived.

INVITE THE SPOUSES OF LOCAL CANDIDATES AND LOCAL CANDIDATES THEMSELVES INTO YOUR SALON FOR FREE SALON SERVICES.

4 Make sure you always have a decent camera on hand, loaded with film. That's an absolute. When a candidate or spouse says they'd like to come by in fifteen minutes or an hour, welcome them with open arms. Don't worry about them wanting to come in on a Saturday. Just as you're too busy, they are also too busy. Make room in your schedule, and be waiting for them when they arrive. Chances are they'll just want some simple sort of refresher service. During the election season they scarcely have time for such things as a "Day of Beauty." When the service is completed, take several photos of the candidate or candidate's spouse together with the appropriate stylist and, *always*, you. Have an 8 x 10 photo sent to each candidate or spouse.

5 On the morning after Election Day, put up a big sign in your window that says, CONGRATULATIONS! Under it put a photo of each of the winning candidates and/or their spouses, together with a hand-lettered sign identifying each person. Leave the display in your window for about a week or so. Everyone who passes by will surely be interested in these photographs and will surely be impressed that these people were done in your salon.

6 If you feel like springing for a little advertising, pick the candidate (and/or spouse) who was worked on in your salon and got elected to whatever the highest office is. Just do a congratulatory ad as though you are congratulating one of your favorite clients on their election.

During the course of these pre-Election Day activities you will have made a lot of new friends and met a lot of locally important people. Who knows? You may even have impressed them enough for them to become steady clients. Your own clients will be delighted because everyone loves to rub shoulders with important people. They'll like saying, "I go to the same salon as the new supervisor."

After you do this whole activity one time, you'll learn a lot about local election activity, party activity, campaigning schedules, and candidates' habits. Use all this knowledge to do the exact same promotion next year— but with all the improvements you've made due to your new experience and knowledge.

Everyone loves a winner. And with this promotion, your salon will always be on the winning side.

DURING THE COURSE OF

THESE PRE-ELECTION

DAY ACTIVITIES YOU

WILL HAVE MADE A LOT

OF NEW FRIENDS AND

MET A LOT OF LOCALLY

IMPORTANT PEOPLE.

Hair Services "Packages" During the Holiday Season

HOLIDAY

DISCOUNT OFFER

Combination packages—grouping together several hair care services for one special combination price—are a good idea all year long, but they may not "hit home" during most of the year. The holiday season, the period from just before Thanksgiving right up until New Year's Eve, is a very special time. People are more expansive and more generous. They're happier at this time of year. They're more willing to spend money at this time of year, and, perhaps most important of all, they really want to look good for their many holiday events and get-togethers. So they're especially wide open and susceptible to giving themselves a special treat. The treat you should offer is a combination package.

You'll always want to include a shampoo, haircut, blowout, and conditioning in the combination. Everyone always needs those. What else you include is totally up to you and what services are available in your salon. A mini-highlighting would certainly be a candidate. They're easy to do and nonthreatening. A fifteen-minute therapeutic scalp massage is always a mouth waterer. Manicure services are always in order. Do you offer waxing? The whole service costs very little, takes very little time, and always produces happy results. Skin care services, facial treatments? They're just the kind of luxuries clients may be willing to give themselves during the holiday season. Do you have any talented makeup people on your staff? How about a fifteen-minute makeup lesson?

PEOPLE REALLY WANT TO LOOK GOOD FOR THEIR HOLIDAY EVENTS AND GET-TOGETHERS.

You can see what the psychology is here. You start with something basic that every needs, then you include another two or three services that they might ordinarily not get. Put them all together, make them available at a special price, and—voilà!—you've got a combination package. Here's what you do.

1 You needn't offer just one package. You can easily have a few. Sit yourself down one day, and list every service available in your salon and the price.

2 Group together various services that you think your clientele would find interesting.

3 You may decide to offer the various packages at various price levels. There could be a $50 package, a $75 package, a $100 package, all the way up to whatever combination price you would want to charge for "The Works."

4 Starting in October, post signs in your salon about the availability of your package(s). Clients who come in for appointments during the September/October period will surely be coming back again during the Thanksgiving/Christmas/New Year's period. When they see your combination prices, many will book themselves.

5 Make sure that whoever takes appointments on the phone knows the combination packages backward and forward. When a client calls in to book one or another of the basic services that's on one of your combinations, the booking person can easily say, "Oh, Mrs. Jones, we'll have a special combination package available on the day of your appointment. For only an additional [XX] dollars you can have all the services in Combination B." She will, of course, say what the services are and what the savings will be. A sharp booking person will be able to trade up most of the basic appointments into one or another of the combination packages.

At the end of the holiday season the salon will have done many, many more services than would normally be the case when simply booking clients for it's standard services. Many of these services will be relatively new to many of the clients. Let's take for granted that the services were all performed to the clients' satisfaction. All of this translates into a raft of additional services performed on your regular clientele all throughout the year.

COMBINATION PACKAGES TRANSLATE INTO A RAFT OF ADDITIONAL SERVICES PERFORMED ON YOUR REGULAR CLIENTELE THROUGHOUT THE YEAR.

Discount Cards As
Christmas Favors

Christmas favors are always a problem. The question first arises as to whether or not you should give out Christmas favors at all. In most salons, the dilemma is solved in the affirmative. Salon owners usually elect to give clients some sort of little gift during the holiday season. *What* to give then becomes the problem. If it's a little trinket like an imprinted comb or plastic rain bonnet, it almost has no meaning. A very excellent idea is to give some sort of gift that will not only be meaningful but may indeed bring some business to the salon. There's a way to do it that will a) be appreciated, b) increase your retail business, c) bring clients into the salon at a normally slow time. The plan is to give a discount gift card for the purchase of retail merchandise as your Christmas favor. Here's how to work it.

HOLIDAY

PRINTED MATERIAL

DISCOUNT OFFER

1 Have cards printed that say on the front:

HOLIDAY GREETINGS

and a

HOLIDAY GIFT

from your friends at Beauty Unlimited

You can print your message in a straightforward fashion or you can use photos or beauty themes as a background.

2 On the inside of the card convey a message something like:

All of us at Beauty Unlimited extend our Best Wishes for a Happy Holiday Season and a Happy New Year.

In the Spirit of the season we'd like to extend this gift of a

50 percent DISCOUNT

on any hair care product we carry in our salon. Simply present this 50 percent discount card at any time between now and January 31st, select your product and take 50 percent off the price.

AN EXCELLENT

CHRISTMAS FAVOR

IS A GIFT THAT'S

MEANINGFUL AND

BRINGS IN BUSINESS.

NOTES

3 Have these cards printed up in a size that approximates regular Christmas cards. People don't consider holiday greetings cards as junk mail. They open and read each and every card. You can be absolutely assured that your thoughtful message will be read by every individual on your mailing list.

4 Don't mail the cards too early in the holiday season. You're probably busy during the month of December and usually don't need any special devices to pull people in. December 20th would be a good time to put the cards in the mail.

Most of the "redemptions" will then take place in the month of January. Some people may just come in, pick a product, and take their discounts. Many more, however, will come in and really look over your range of retail products before they make their selection. This will familiarize them with the different lines and products and will enable you or your staff to talk about product characteristics. Chances are they'll buy one of the products at the discount and buy one or two more at the regular prices. Others will do even better. They'll actually schedule January appointments they might not normally have.

You may be concerned that the promotion will cost you too much. It really won't. Let's take a relatively expensive product, a $10 shampoo. Normally it would cost you $5, so when you're giving your 50 percent discount on the sale, you will have gotten your money back. It won't cost you anything. At the same time, many clients will be trying products they never used before. If they're pleased with the results—and why shouldn't they be?—the profits will come on the repeat business. No matter how extensive a retail business you do, the fact is that a great many of your clients buy absolutely no hair care products from you. The discount gift card will have everybody at least trying various types of your exclusively professional retail products.

5 Be absolutely certain to sit down with your distributors and/or their sales people who call on you. Tell them what your plans are. Tell them you will be selling a significant amount of hair care products at this deep, deep discount and that you solicit their cooperation. Why should they be making their full 40 percent profit on the discounted merchandise while you make nothing? Ask for a 20 percent discount on the merchandise you buy during December and January, especially on the popular, fast-moving products most clients will select. The same $10 shampoo that normally costs you $5 and that you'll be selling at the $5 discount price will only cost $4 if your distributor gives you a 20 percent discount. He'll still be making a profit, his volume will increase, and you'll make a modest profit that will pay for your printing and postage costs. Don't be shy about this. When your distributor runs some special promotion, he often gets special consideration from the manufacturer. No reason why you shouldn't expect the same. You'll be surprised how cooperative most distributors will be.

If it turns out that this whole idea is happily accepted by your clients, and if it increases your retail business generally, don't wait until next year to try variations of it. All retail establishments constantly work and rework promotional deals and discounts. You can recycle this with different discount levels or specific products as birthday, anniversary, graduation, back-to-school promotions. Learn from every promotion. What works should be recycled; what doesn't, discarded. Take an idea from this promotion, combine it with an idea from another. Always think promotionally. And what better time can there be than the end of one year and the beginning of another.

LEARN FROM EVERY PROMOTION. WHAT WORKS SHOULD BE RECYCLED; WHAT DOESN'T, DISCARDED.

A Christmas Promotion to Build Your Makeup Business

HOLIDAY

PRINTED MATERIAL

It's the custom in many salons to give a gift to clients who come in during the December holiday season. This lovely idea helps the bonding process between client and salon. Often the big problem is what to give. Salon owners have given little calendars, imprinted combs, or sample sizes of beauty or fragrance products. All fine. The best idea, however, is to give a gift that can actually build business. A sample size of a retail product is certainly one way of doing this. Another, and perhaps even better, idea is to give clients a service they virtually never choose for themselves but may enjoy so much that they'll want to repeat either the full service or the products connected with this service again and again. Such a service would be an eye makeup makeover.

What a delight! Most women have an abundance of eye makeup products in their cabinets but a definite insufficiency of confidence as to how to use them for maximum effect. So by doing an eye makeup makeover, you'll be filling an absolute need—and your clients will appreciate it.

BY DOING AN EYE MAKEUP MAKEOVER, YOU'LL BE FILLING AN ABSOLUTE NEED— AND YOUR CLIENTS WILL APPRECIATE IT.

Before going into the nuts and bolts of this kind of Christmas promotion, you must determine who if anyone in your salon is truly competent in analyzing a client's bone structure, facial composition, and needs regarding her eye makeup. If someone's just going to slap makeup on, no good. The client can do that herself. The people assigned to this task must really know what they're doing. If your staff isn't up to the task, it's an urgent signal to start practicing.

Schedule after-hours workshops and clinics. Get your distributor to send in a makeup expert from one of the companies he represents. The appropriate people should practice, work on it, play with it, have fun with it, become expert at it. Some of the junior people in the salon, the ones who aren't booked to capacity, would be the ideal people to become the Christmas makeup practitioners. Once you're satisfied that you have experts who will be available, you're ready to start your promotion.

1 This essentially will *not* be a promotion to attract new clients. It's a promotion to build the salon's relationship with existing clients and boost the makeup service and sale of makeup products. So you need to gather

your list of current clients—women who have been in your salon for services within the last six months to a year.

2 Immediately after Thanksgiving, mail out your Christmas card. It can be a special preprinted card that contains your Christmas greetings plus the offer of your special holiday gift. Or you can send out standard Christmas cards and enclose a printed insert that says "Our Gift To You."

3 Your gift will be an eye makeup application, consisting of the removal of any eye makeup she may currently have on, then the application of mascara, shadow, liner, and pencil. The process takes anywhere from ten to fifteen minutes, so make sure you allow for it in scheduling appointments.

4 Don't restrict the eye makeup gift to the holiday season. In fact, since your salon is fairly heavily booked in the month of December, make sure to extend redemption of the gift through the full month of January. This will also be subtle and unspoken reminder to the client that she ought to book an appointment during January.

5 When the client books her regular appointment and informs the person on the phone that she would also like to schedule her eye makeup session, she should be told to bring all her eye makeup products with her so that her makeup artist may use (and therefore teach her how to use) her existing products. Here's where the opportunity for multiple eye product sales will be absolutely glorious.

THE OPPORTUNITY FOR MULTIPLE EYE PRODUCT SALES WILL BE ABSOLUTELY GLORIOUS.

a) When the client plops down her array of products, it will be immediately apparent that some are many months old. It's a matter of absolute truth that many eye infections are brought about as a result of using old bacteria-contaminated products. Anything more than three or four months old should be discarded. This creates an immediate void in the client's supply—a void you can easily fill.

b) The shades the client has in her inventory may be appropriate for her complexion and the effects she wishes to achieve—or they may *not* be appropriate. If the latter, she will automatically want to buy the right shades.

c) The client often won't have all the products she really should have to do a really effective job. Obviously you can solve this problem by suggesting she should have the missing products.

d) During the entire eye makeup procedure, the cosmetologist will be talking—not merely about products and shades but about the

THE FREEBIE EYE

MAKEUPS YOU

DO DURING THE

MONTHS OF DECEMBER

AND JANUARY WILL

ESTABLISH YOU AND

YOUR SALON PEOPLE AS

THE EXPERTS.

superiority of the makeup line you carry. Will this cause some clients to switch from their brand to yours? Goes without saying.

Many salons have surrendered makeup sales to supermarkets, drugstore chains, and department stores. Food and drugstores sell products at the lower end of the price spectrum, department stores sell the pricey brands. The primary way department stores make new sales is by their willingness, eagerness, to demonstrate. Once a woman sits down in that chair, it's a foregone conclusion that she will buy products. Often enough a bystander or two who has been watching will make a purchase, as well. The freebie eye makeups you do during the months of December and January will establish you and your salon people as the experts. You will sell more eye products than you can imagine and have a lot of happy women feeling kindly toward your salon because of your gracious gift.

Salon Birthday Promotion

Promo 22

HOLIDAY

PRINTED MATERIAL

There are, of course, many ways to celebrate birthdays. Understandably, most of them celebrate the birthdays of clients. I know a salon owner who pulled a switch on that idea. He opened his salon in a new strip mall, and his first year was quite a struggle, but he managed to make it through. Some of the other merchants did not. He was so pleased at having survived that he decided to have a birthday celebration *for the salon*! Here are some of the things he did to make it a successful promotion:

1 A month before the salon's actual birthday he had two signs made up, one for inside the salon and one for the salon window. They said:

OUR 1ST BIRTHDAY!

FREE BIRTHDAY CAKE TO ALL ON JUNE 15TH

YOU NEEDN'T BE OUR CLIENT

We Want to Celebrate With Everyone

So Come On In On June 15th

FREE Birthday Cake And Fruit Juice

2 During the entire month before the birthday, each client was reminded of the date on the way out. Many promised to come in, and, indeed, many did. In addition, passersby definitely came in, as well.

3 The owner ordered a large sheet cake suitably decorated, and several gallons of various juices were on hand. He figured that if there was any cake left over, it could be divided among the staff, and juice could be kept in the refrigerator and used over time. It turned out that before the day was over, they just about ran out of cake and had to replenish the supply of juice from the local supermarket.

Did it bring in any new business? Maybe yes, maybe no, but it certainly told everybody in and around that shopping mall that that salon was there and that they were friendly folks willing to share a happy occasion.

4 That's not the end of the story. The owner did the same thing again the next year—and the next and the next—and it really got to be a tradition. Clients got to asking about it and looking forward to it. Nearby merchants always dropped in, and many strangers, including a lot of young people, invariably showed up, too. The annual birthday celebration essentially conveyed the message, without saying it in so many words: "We're good, we've lasted all these years, we must be doing something right." And many of the non-clients who just pop in for a free piece of birthday cake and a cup of juice later wind up becoming clients.

You have to realize that no matter how loyal a client is to any particular salon, there can come a time when she either gets tired of it or gets annoyed with something or other and is ready to try another salon. If she's at least familiar with the interior of another salon and the friendliness and neighborliness of another salon, gravity will take her there.

Some of the young teens who come by just to freeload eventually graduate from their teens. They may join the workforce and need beauty services. Who will they consider favorably? Their friends, the birthday people.

You can even keep your costs down by bartering services with the bakery. If they don't want to do that, ask if they'd like to have a sign next to the cake telling where it came from. Of course, that plug merits a discount.

Whenever you can create a happy atmosphere in your salon, you're building business, no doubt about it. And what could be happier than a birthday party?

The Mother of
All Salon Promotions

Promo
23

BIRTHDAYS! Salon owners have been doing birthday promotions for years, decades. They've been so popular that some folks have felt they're a bit tired, so many salons have cut them out. Don't fall into this trap! A thing that's worth doing is worth doing again. The reason so many salons have done birthday promotions is that they're easy and they work! Remember, we're living in an age where there is less and less service, less and less personalized attention. Most stores and most malls are run by kids who just don't care. At a time when people are becoming numbers rather than names, who wouldn't like to receive a birthday remembrance on their birthday, especially from the salon they visit all year long?

HOLIDAY

PRINTED MATERIAL

WHO WOULDN'T
LIKE TO RECEIVE A
REMEMBRANCE ON
THEIR BIRTHDAY?

On any person's birthday, the mailbox contains several cards, maybe a few gifts. This is not junk mail. People open each card and read it. They'll read your card. They'll be grateful that you remembered, and they'll be thrilled if some kind of gift is involved. So let's organize a birthday promotion.

1 The first thing you must have is everyone's birth date. You should already have this information in your records, but if you don't, start accumulating it right now. From now on, when a new client comes in, you should ask for her name, address, phone number, and birth date at the very least. There may be many other things you'll want to know about individual clients, but for purposes of a birthday promotion, we're only interested in the date.

2 When you ask for a client's birth date, let her know that the month and the day are important, but the year is not. Some may be willing to share that, some won't. For this promotion, the year makes no difference.

3 If you have a computer database set up, programming the dates sequentially will be a simple matter. If you don't have a computer, gather the information on 3 x 5 index cards.

4 You may have the kind of information cards that list the dates the client came in, what services were done, what her haircolor formula is, and so on. You may already have her address and birth date listed on these cards. You doubtless keep these cards in alphabetical order. That's as it should be, but for purposes of a birthday promotion, you really need the cards in a completely different order—chronologically. Therefore, you ought to keep a separate set of cards that has just names, addresses, and birth dates kept in strict chronological order.

5 Buy fifty-two index tabs and put the cards you've listed everyone's birthday on into the fifty-two sequential weeks of the year.

6 Set aside a specific time each week when you, your manager, your receptionist, your shampoo person, or whoever is assigned to this task sits down, takes out the week's cards, and addresses them.

7 In the absolutely simplest form of any birthday promotion, simply send a birthday greeting card to each of your clients. This alone will help business. They'll appreciate your thoughtfulness and consideration, and that can only help your relationship with each client.

8 Actually, it is best not simply to extend your greetings but to sweeten them up a bit with a birthday gift. It can be a free piece of merchandise, a birthday "goodie bag" with several sample sizes of product you carry, or a service of some sort.

THE GIFT THAT MAKES THE MOST SENSE IS TO OFFER A SERVICE THAT YOU'RE TRYING TO BUILD IN THE SALON.

9 The gift that makes the most sense is to offer a service that you're trying to build in the salon. Are you just starting to promote nail services? Offer a free manicure or a hot wax treatment. Newly into skin care? Say Happy Birthday with a free facial treatment. The client will collapse with gratitude. A scalp massage may thrill her so that she'll book future treatments. You get the idea.

10 Of course, you can offer standard services such as haircuts, but if she's a fairly regular client, she'll be coming in for those anyway. We want to get her into services she may not be into, services you're trying to build.

11 If you have the time, you can actually invite her in for the free service or product with a handwritten note right on the card. In most cases this is too time consuming, so it's best to have a specially printed card that gives her all the necessary information. You don't have to sign a printed card, although it's certainly nice to do so.

12 If you do print the card, it can say something like this:

HAPPY BIRTHDAY!

At the Magic Fingers Beauty Salon we love happy occasions—
and your birthday is one of them. Come in soon so that we
can offer our birthday greetings in person and give you a
birthday gift we know you'll love . . .
A fifteen-minute therapeutic scalp massage with our
compliments!
So schedule an appointment soon, and please bring this card
with you.
Have a wonderful birthday. We look forward to seeing you
soon.
Magic Fingers Salon • Brookwood Plaza • Milford, NY •
Tel. 567-3333

13 When the client comes in, make sure that you, as the salon owner, are alerted in advance so that you can personally greet her. On a selective basis you can also give an additional gift, perhaps a retail product as a special present from you. It's a nice personal gesture.

Many things go into the overall process of keeping clients happy, and we all know what many of them are. But one of the most important is an ongoing personal relationship between not only the stylist and the client but the owner and client and the entire salon and the client. Remembering birthdays is surely one of the absolutely best ways you can keep this personal relationship going.

The Classic Birthday Promotion

HOLIDAY

PRINTED MATERIAL

PROBABLY THE MOST

FREQUENTLY USED

SALON PROMOTION

IS THE BIRTHDAY

PROMOTION AND WITH

GOOD REASON: IT

ALWAYS WORKS.

Probably the most frequently used salon promotion is the birthday promotion and with good reason: It always works. There are all sorts of variations on this promotion, and you'll find others in other parts of this book. But the classic is still the give-her-a-free-gift-on-her-birthday promotion.

Even though it's lovely promotion and an easy one, you still have to give it thought, and you still have to be organized about it.

1 You should have the birth date of every client who walks through your door on record. Some salons ask new clients to fill in an information form such as doctors use on the first visit. Others simply ask each client their birth date and record it in a book. In either case, make sure the client knows that you only want the month and day of her birth. Your records should contain not only each and every client's date of birth but also her name, address, and phone number. Whether you use a computer database, a set of index cards, or simply a notebook, keep all the birth dates chronologically by month and day.

2 Two or three weeks before the client's actual birthday, send her a postcard, a letter, a birthday card, or whatever. The main thing you want her to know is that you're aware that her birthday is coming up in a couple of weeks, and you want her to know that she has a *free gift* waiting for her at the salon.

3 The gift should *not* be a piece of merchandise. It should be a service. You may do a lot of retailing in your salon, but the percentage of retail business you do is certainly minor compared to the percentage of service business. You don't want to celebrate her birthday by her popping in one day, picking up a free tube of something or other, and saying, "Sayonara." No, you want her to come into the salon for a specific service.

4 The birthday card or letter should go out to every person who had any sort of service in your salon in the past year. Many of these will still be clients, and they'll be absolutely delighted at your generosity in offering them a free service. But some of the recipients of the cards or letters will

be people who've stopped coming to the salon for one reason or another. They're the ones you want to woo back. If you manage to make a good enough second impression on some of these folks, and they start coming to the salon again, your whole birthday promotion outlay will be more than paid for.

5 What service to give as a birthday present? Cuts, colors, and perms are not advisable. The client may be letting her hair grow and might not want to cut it for months. She may not be coloring her hair, or may not want to, so a haircolor gift will go unused. Perms? Very touchy. A lot of people simply don't want them, so your gift will be meaningless. Ah, but how about nail services? Everybody can use a manicure or some nail extensions. A facial treatment, if the service is available in your salon, is a gift not one client will be able to resist. How about a fifteen-minute therapeutic scalp massage? They'll flock!

6 You'll find that a great percentage of the recipients will automatically book themselves for another service or two. If the service you give away introduces them to something they'd normally not have done in the salon, you've got a very good chance of building a whole new area of business simply by being nice and generous and remembering people's birthdays.

7 Want to make it even warmer, lovelier, more appreciated, more fun? Do what they do in restaurants. In the middle of the service, bring over a cupcake with one birthday candle on it, and have a group of stylists converge around the client, then—all together now—sing "Happy Birthday to You."

Put yourself in your client's shoes. If you were treated this way by your salon, wouldn't that greatly solidify your relationship with them? Or if you were a former client who came back just for the free birthday service, wouldn't it warm your heart and melt your resistance to returning to the salon?

The friendliness, generosity, and high spirits that surround the entire birthday promotion will surely even impress other clients in the salon who are not celebrating their birthdays. It's all pluses and no minuses. And that's why the classic birthday promotion is more popular than any other used in salons.

YOU'VE GOT A GOOD CHANCE TO BUILD A NEW AREA OF BUSINESS SIMPLY BY BEING GENEROUS FOR PEOPLE'S BIRTHDAYS.

Eliminating the "Stigma" of Senior Citizen Days

EVENT

HOLIDAY

DISCOUNT OFFER

Many retailers have found that giving special discounts and incentives to senior citizens turns out to be good business. Often the incentives are given only one or two days a week—usually the days that stores experience the lowest sales and/or lowest traffic. Then, too, it's kind of a civic-minded thing to do to welcome seniors, whose numbers have grown and will continue to grow.

On the other hand, some salons are reluctant to engage in this kind of promotional activity. They feel they may get an "old lady image." We've got to organize an activity that will destroy any senior-citizen image problem.

1 A great way to establish a positive image is to structure your promotion so that it's very specifically geared to *teenagers* as well as senior citizens. Remember that when kids have trouble with adults, it's usually in their parents' age group. On the other hand, they generally have a mutual love affair with their grandparents. So inviting teenagers in on the same days (usually early in the week) as seniors can make everybody happy. When you've got both the kids *and* older folks coming in, there's surely no possibility of anyone thinking you have an "old lady salon."

2 You can get the word out by a simple but professionally done window sign announcing that on Tuesdays and Wednesdays (or whatever days you wish) anyone in their teens or who's 60 and older will receive a special incentive for booking appointments on those days. The incentives can be discounts of anywhere up to 50 percent or perhaps a free nail service with every hair service or maybe offer a free retail product.

3 How slow you are during the early part of the week will determine how generous you should make your offer. If Tuesdays are absolutely dead, why not get people in at half-price? On the other hand, if business is decent early in the week but just a bit slower than it is later on, you can be less generous.

ORGANIZE AN ACTIVITY

THAT WILL DESTROY

ANY SENIOR-CITIZEN

IMAGE PROBLEM.

When participating in this kind of promotion, all stylists should be mindful that when a teenager is sitting in their chair, it certainly would be appropriate to ask them to suggest that they tell their grandmother about the great early-in-the-week deal. Similarly, many of the grandparents will have multiple grandchildren. So when a grandmother is in the chair, it's perfectly sensible to encourage her to suggest that her grandchildren come in for the teens 'n seniors special prices.

You'll find that these two particular generations actually like each other and want to help each other. By promoting their patronage in your salon, you're actually encouraging closer family interplay.

Here Comes the Bride—And the Entire Wedding Party

EVENT

HOLIDAY

DISCOUNT OFFER

A LOT OF BEAUTY WORK

GETS DONE JUST FOR A

SINGLE WEDDING.

A lot of beauty work gets done just for a single wedding. Consider that we have the bride and groom and both sets of parents. Then there's the maid of honor and best man. There may be four or more bridesmaids and their escorts. Now we have sixteen people even before we get to the guest list— which can add another hundred people. That's a lot of cuts, colors, stylings, manicures, makeups, and on and on. That's the good news. The bad news is that these one hundred and two hundred people are dispersed geographically so that several dozen salons each get their own tiny piece of the pie. It would be to ambitious and virtually impossible to capture everybody, but let's at least try to get a bigger slice of the business. Here's the plan:

1   While June is the big wedding month, remember that people get married twelve months a year, so we want to have a promotional framework that's ongoing with no beginning and no end.

2   We need the names of brides, whether they are currently salon clients or not. Some local newspapers publish listings of all couples who apply for a marriage license. Get those names. By personal conversation with every client in the salon, on an ongoing basis, solicit the names of people who have gotten engaged or are planning to get married. Have a little fun with it. Tell the clients that if they're the first to notify you of an impending wedding, they can have their pick of any product in the salon for free.

3   The minute you get the name and address of a bride within reasonable proximity of your salon, call or write her. Congratulate her and invite her and/or her mother to the salon for a free shampoo, style, blowout, and manicure. Explain that you'd like to do other members of the wedding party, and you'd like her (and possibly her mother) to see the quality of the salon, experience the level of work and service you perform, and hear about your Bridal Party Program.

4 Formulate your Bridal Party Program so that you can discuss it with the bride when she comes in. Every wedding is different. Every salon is different. You'll have to come up with your own program. Here are some things you might consider:

- Tell the bride to suggest your salon to everyone in the official wedding party as well as to all friends and relatives who may attend. Have the bride tell these people to mention that they are going to her wedding, which will qualify them for a 20 percent discount on all services. Don't worry that you're "giving away the store." Most of these folks will be new clients, and it will be a glorious opportunity to impress them.

- Give the bride a little extra bonus. If ten people who are attending the wedding book appointments, do the bride for free. (If this hurts too much make it a 50 percent discount. Obviously none of these points are written in stone. Change them at your will.)

- If several people in the wedding party want to book all at once, arrange for special evening hours where the shop is totally devoted to the needs of the wedding party.

- Make yourself or others you designate available at the site of the wedding on the wedding day—at whatever fee you feel is fair. Brides love this. Last minute makeups, combings, and finishing touches give the wedding a Hollywood flair.

5 If a group of guests are coming from out of town and are all staying at a local hotel/motel, offer to send a stylist and nail artist there to do freshen-ups and manicures the night before the wedding. Each will pay her own bill—or perhaps the bride will pick up the whole tab as a courtesy.

6 Always have pictures taken of the bride in finished form and in the process of being styled. Once you have photographs of a half dozen or more weddings, mount them on a sign in the salon under the heading:

WE SPECIALIZE IN BRIDES

ASK ABOUT OUR BRIDAL PARTY PROGRAM

YOUR SALON'S WORK WILL BE ON DISPLAY BEFORE MAYBE A COUPLE OF HUNDRED PEOPLE.

There are salons who believe in charging premium prices when they are "on location" at the brides home, church, or hotel. That's fine if it works for you, but remember that with all the money being expended on the wedding, the bride and her family may be more attracted by discount rather than premium prices. Your salon's work will be on display before maybe a couple of hundred people. If the bride and her party look glorious, if the styles are beautiful, if the hair is perfectly colored and conditioned, there *will* be talk; it *will* be noticed. That talk and that notice will directly translate into new clients and new dollars for your salon.

The Revenge of the Football Widows

EVENT

YOU CAN MAKE A LOT

OF NEW FRIENDS

AND BOOK A LOT OF

NEW BUSINESS ON

SUPERBOWL SUNDAY.

For a depressingly large portion of our population, Superbowl Sunday is the most important day of the year. It's basically a man's holiday: They talk about it for weeks before and make plans for the Big Day. They gather in groups at someone's house or a local bar. They consume oceans of beer and mountains of popcorn, potato chips, crackers, and pretzels. In the last few years, women have become interested, but in many cases it's a defensive tactic. They hang around or come along to watch and participate because if they don't, they're utterly ignored and deserted for the day. These are the women who figure, "I can't beat 'em, so I may as well join 'em." But joining them does not confer acceptance. The men still mostly cheer, argue, and shout with each other while the women in the room are tolerated rather than accepted.

But we are living in an era where women are aggressive and assertive, and I know some who have fought back—and won. If you're a salon owner who has very little interest in football, you can be one of these women and make a lot of new friends and book a lot of new business on Superbowl Sunday. Here's what you do.

1 Find yourself a dress-shop owner who carries great lines of clothes, who's entrepreneurial, and who has as little interest in football as you do. Have dinner with her, and over a glass of wine make your plans.

2 You have a fairly extensive list of female clients. She has an equally extensive list of female customers. That's a lot of women who may share your mutual disdain for the whole Superbowl phenomenon.

3 Plan a beauty, makeup, and fashion event that day, either at the dress shop or your salon. Pick whichever space will allow you to have the most seating and a decent runway area. If your salon's space is appropriate, schedule the event there. It will generate more business for you.

4 What you'll be doing is putting on a show that will display the clothing your friend the dress-shop owner wants to show and the skills, abilities, and services available in your salon that you'll want to show. Superbowl time is an appropriate time to show upcoming spring and summer fashions and cruise wear. On your part, you can show new cuts, styles, color and perm techniques, and even nail artistry.

5 Serve champagne and some finger food. This will add to the festivities, joyful atmosphere, and the loosening of purse strings.

6 You and the dress-shop owner will introduce yourselves, and she'll describe an opening set of fashions accompanied by appropriate models. Then you and your team will come on and show some beautiful finished hairstyles and colors and perhaps do a haircut on someone from the audience. Then more fashions and more models, after which you and your team will perform and display other services. And that's the way it will go—fashions and hairstyles, fashions and hairstyles, until you fill up the allotted time.

7 Be certain to leave plenty of time for questions and answers. You, particularly, will be getting a lot of them about techniques, procedures, products, facts, myths, customs, and so on. This is your opportunity to charm the audience and subtly convey to them what a pleasurable, stress-free experience a visit to your salon will be.

8 There's the matter of models. The dress-shop owner will doubtlessly have some she is accustomed to using. You'll have your own stylists and special clients who'll be willing to participate. If all else fails, there's the audience. In a room full of women, there are always several who are willing to volunteer their heads for free services.

9 Makeovers are always effective. You should plan on two or three in advance. Got a video camera? Videotape them "before." You can do the actual makeover during your demonstration and the videotaped "before" shots compared to the finished actual models will be dramatic.

10 Attendance at your show should be by invitation only. The invitations can be via personal conversations you have with your clients and your dress-shop friend has with her customers. Or you can both do a mailing, but that may elicit a greater response than you have capacity for. Your best bet will be to put a sign in your salon and a sign in her shop: WHILE THEY'RE DRINKING BEER, WE'LL BE HAVING CHAMPAGNE would be a nice tagline.

FOOTBALL OR FASHION? TAKE YOUR CHOICE! would be another possibility. THEY CHEER, WE SHOP would be a third. You can see the possibility for fun.

11 The dress-shop owner will do more business than you at the show. She's got actual merchandise, you've got invitations to make appointments. Don't fret. You'll get your appointments—especially if you've done lovely, practical, fashionable, up-to-the-minute work.

12 To encourage appointments, have a supply of your salon's business cards with you. In advance, on each of these write **25 percent Courtesy Discount**. Then sign your name. Tell the ladies about this special one-shot offer, and invite them in. Some will want to schedule appointments right then. Others will call within the next couple of weeks. Make sure you get everyone's address and phone number. That way you can get on the phone with those you haven't heard from and remind them that the 25 percent courtesy discount will expire [XX] days after the show. That will result in still more appointments.

13 What will make your show the talk of the town is if you can get some press, radio, or local TV coverage. The two of you should make personal telephone or mail contact with the beauty editors and sports editors. Call the local TV station if you have one. This is a great human-interest story, and they may jump on it.

The best part of all this is that you'll mingle with a whole bunch of women who feel that they will actually be expressing themselves by attending your beauty, makeup, and fashion show. They may even be motivated by a "revenge factor" of wanting to go out, have a good time, and splurge a little for the times they were kept on the fringes of Superbowl festivities. It will be a "liberation day" of sorts, and you'll be one of the liberators. Won't that be nice?

IT WILL BE A "LIBERATION DAY" OF SORTS, AND YOU'LL BE ONE OF THE LIBERATORS.

When You Go to a Show, Merchandise It

EVENT

Whether you know it or not, your clients look to you for the latest in hair fashions, techniques, and products. They may get information from the women's fashion and service magazines, but this information is distant. They don't know quite what to do with it, how to benefit from it. But when information comes from you, they know it can be translated directly to their benefit.

Make no mistake about it, clients *want* this information. They're eager for it. When it's forthcoming from you, they appreciate it and are impressed by it. They want you to be up on the very latest in hair. They may elect not to take your advice or suggestions, but they still want you to have the knowledge to give this advice and these suggestions. Here's how to keep your clients informed that *you* are informed.

1 Simple postcards constitute one of the best ways to let all your clients know that you are keeping up with the latest in fashion and technology. Do you go to any of the major shows—the International Beauty Show, the MidWest Beauty Show, the Long Beach Beauty Show? Tell your clients about it. Send them each a postcard from New York, Chicago, or Long Beach. It can say something like:

> "Hi—I'm in New York attending the International Beauty Show. It's fantastic. I'm learning about the latest in hair fashions, techniques, and products. I'll tell you all about them when I get back."

2 Obviously, you can change the copy to suit your own personality, your own circumstances, your own clientele. If you go with a group from the salon, you can talk about what "we're" learning, and you can sign it "Your friends at Such-and-Such Salon."

3 The postcards should be of the picture variety, showing one of the tourist sights in the host city. When your client gets it, she will read it. She won't toss it away without a glance the way she does much of her junk mail. And she'll appreciate it and be impressed by it. Indeed, she'll probably ask you about your trip during her very next appointment.

WHETHER YOU KNOW IT OR NOT, YOUR CLIENTS LOOK TO YOU FOR THE LATEST IN HAIR FASHIONS, TECHNIQUES, AND PRODUCTS.

4 If you're only going to send postcards to a limited number of your clients, you can buy them in the host city, and write them up right there. If you want to send them to the salon's entire clientele, you'll have to buy them one year for the next. Or have a friend who lives in the host city buy the cards for you and send them to you ahead of time.

5 If you intend to write to all clients, you can actually write the message on one card, then bring it to a printer who'll duplicate it with blue ink just as though each card was handwritten.

Even if the subject doesn't come up when you get back from shows, your clients will be impressed that you're keeping up with the latest—and that you thought of them while you were away.

6 Maybe you don't like the postcard idea, but you do like the concept of telling your clients about your attendance at the show. Put up a sign in the window saying something like:

WE'RE OFF TO NEW YORK CITY, MARCH 15–18, TO LEARN THE LATEST
AT THE INTERNATIONAL BEAUTY SHOW.

When you come back, replace it with a sign that says something like:

WE'RE BACK FROM THE INTERNATIONAL BEAUTY SHOW IN NEW YORK
CITY. WE SAW AND LEARNED THE LATEST. COME ON IN.

You can use all these devices not only when you attend the big shows in New York, Chicago, or Long Beach, but when you attend any kind of show. If you go to Haircolor USA, tell your clients about it. If you attend the International Haircolor Exchange, let everybody know. If you attend several events during the course of the year, write your clients a postcard each time. The effect will be cumulative. Clients will even start to brag about you ("My hairstylist just came back from a big show and she says everybody's doing . . .").

Wouldn't you like to know that your doctor is attending medical conferences, seminars, and lectures to keep up with the latest medications and techniques in his specialty? Of course you would. That's just the way your clients will feel about news that you are always learning, always keeping up.

CLIENTS LIKE TO KNOW THAT YOU ARE ALWAYS LEARNING, ALWAYS KEEPING UP.

Tie In with "Bring Your Daughter to Work Day"

A wonderful activity that's been taking place for the past several years is a national program called "Bring Your Daughter to Work Day." It was conceived so that little (and not so little) girls are brought into the workplace to see how people make their livings'. It brings families a bit closer and broadens the horizons for young kids. It's a wonderful idea, and if you latch on to it, you get to take advantage of the media publicity that swirls all about that day.

Keep in mind that not all people have employment that lends itself to visiting daughters. Hazardous jobs, bank jobs, high-powered, high-stress jobs, jobs with unsympathetic employers are out. So that one day your salon can be a visiting place, a haven, kind of playland for a certain number of girls whose parents can't take them to work with them. Here's what you can do:

1 Make sure that every girl is accompanied by a parent, male or female.

2 Plan two sessions, one for morning, one for afternoon. Each session will have a short tour of the salon and an introduction to every member of the staff. Make sure you explain that each employee is licensed by the state—same as doctors and lawyers—and each employee has gone through a rigorous schooling and training period. All this ought to take fifteen minutes more or less.

3 Offer either a free haircut or free manicure to every girl in the program, and give every little girl a small gift of shampoo or hand lotion or another piece of appropriate merchandise. (Contact your distributor to see if this merchandise can be made available to you at a very low price, preferably for free.)

4 How many haircutters and nail artists you have will be the determining factor as to how many girls you can accommodate at either the morning session or the afternoon session.

EVENT

PARENT/CHILD

YOUR SALON CAN BE A KIND OF PLAYLAND FOR SOME GIRLS WHOSE PARENTS CAN'T TAKE THEM ON "BRING YOUR DAUGHTER TO WORK DAY."

5 Don't schedule the cuts and manicures for the same length of time it would normally take to handle an adult paying client. Plan for each of the cuts and manicures to take no more than fifteen minutes. Each girl gets a cut *or* manicure, not both.

6 Putting it all together and allowing for some slippage of time in between, schedule the morning session and the afternoon session to take not more than an hour and a half, two hours at the outside.

7 When you have done all the scheduling and figuring, start putting out the word. The first people who should know about your program are your "insiders," your salon clients. Send them each a card explaining your program, and tell them you're booking the number of kids (and their parents) that you can accommodate on a first-come-first-served basis, and they are being notified two weeks before a sign goes up in your window.

8 Start booking for the morning session and the afternoon session. If you fill your quota with clients' kids, that's it. No sign goes up in the window. But if you still have openings, put up that sign saying:

To Celebrate
BRING YOUR DAUGHTER TO WORK DAY
On Such-and-Such Date, 10 [or whatever] **Lucky Little**
Girls Will Receive
FREE HAIRCUTS, *FREE* MANICURES, *FREE* GIFTS
Advanced Registry Required. Details Inside.

9 You, or whomever you designate, should know all the details of the promotion and be able to explain it to any of the men, women, or children who are attracted.

10 Write and/or call your local newspaper's beauty editor, informing her/him of your generous and enlightened gesture to the future women of America. It's a wonderful human-interest story, and the paper may cover it. If they don't bite, make sure you take photos. Send one or two along with a short description of the event to this self-same editor. Truly, local newspapers dote on this sort of thing. There's a better than even chance you'll get some coverage.

What do you get out of this promotion? No, you won't get scads of new clients flocking to your salon, but you will generate an enormous amount of goodwill and good talk. Every client who hears about it, whether they take advantage of it or not, will love you for it. You are doing a gesture for their daughters' generation, and that has to create warm feelings that will ultimately be transformed into salon loyalty and increased business.

Then, too, you'll be attracting a certain number of nonclients. They'll love the idea, they'll see the work you do, and some will surely become clients.

Finally, you don't have to be reminded that time flies. You blink your eyes and that little preteen is going to her junior prom, graduating college, or starting a career. The seeds you planted with those pleasant memories on Bring Your Daughter to Work Day will come to flower when they book their appointments and say, "I remember when I came in here as a little kid."

A Mini Trade Show
for Brides

EVENT

The wedding business is very big business. A lot of people, including perhaps you, make all or part of their living from people getting married. It's also a time when the bride and groom and their immediate families are pretty frazzled from going from one place to another, trying to put together this big theatrical production that will be a wedding. Wouldn't you like to be exposed to all the brides, grooms, bridesmaids, ushers, and others who'll be involved in weddings during the spring and summer "Wedding season?" The way to do it is to organize a show for prospective brides.

1 You've never organized a show before? Not to worry; you're not exactly going to be putting on a Broadway production, and you won't be doing it alone. You'll have lots of help. First, jot down the types of local merchants who are interested in weddings, wedding parties, newlyweds. Some obvious ones are:

GET EXPOSURE TO

BRIDAL PARTIES

BY ORGANIZING

A SHOW FOR

PROSPECTIVE

BRIDES.

Bridal gown shops
Tuxedo rental stores
Florists
Photographers
Furniture stores
Printers
Travel agents
Jewelers
And, or course, beauty salons

2 You may actually know several of these merchants personally. Start with these. Essentially you want to organize them to all chip in an equal amount of money to rent the ballroom (or conference room) of a local hotel/motel for a day, maybe two.

3 Once you have a couple of other merchants lined up, sit down with the person in charge of meetings and shows at the local hotel/motel. He/she will take a good deal of the burden off your hands by telling you what facilities the hotel will provide in terms of lights, partitions, platforms, tables, chairs, and the like.

4 You must sit down and figure out what all this will cost, not only the ballroom, but the refreshments to be served, the ads you'll want to place in the local newspapers, the printing of invitations, and postage. Divide the number you come up with by the number of merchants to determine how much it will cost each of you before you each bring in your own display and/or demonstration material. Assuming you have only one merchant in each category, that will be perhaps a total of nine merchants, so you divide your total costs by nine. You'll all find that it isn't really terribly expensive per merchant, and it's an incredible way to get exposure to every bride in town.

5 If you want to be a little more "liberal" and perhaps have two merchants from each particular category, you'll automatically halve all your costs. Whether you have one merchant from each category or more than one will be up to your group. The likelihood is that none of you will want competitors there, so you'll wind up with only one merchant per category.

6 The decorating of the individual booths will be up to each merchant. In your particular exhibit area you should have one or two styling chairs and have staff members doing cuts, stylings, and consultations all day long. Your job will be to explain your services to anyone and everyone who visits your booth. Prospective brides, grooms, attendants, and parents will wander from exhibit area to exhibit area, and you'll all get a crack at every wedding party on the calendar.

7 In the days or weeks before the show you must come up with a menu of what it is you want to sell. Do you want to assign people to go to the bride's house? Do you want to have a couple of stations in the salon designated exclusively to the wedding party a day before the ceremony? Do you want to offer the services of one of your people at the wedding for last-minute beauty details? Do you want to offer an overall package price for the whole works? Do you want to offer discounts to people who come into the salon and identify themselves as members of the wedding? All these decisions and more are up to you. The main thing is to have everything set down on paper so that when people come into your booth, you can describe all the services that you can make available to the wedding party and what the prices will be. That's what every other merchant will be doing. You must do no less.

8 Make your bridal deal as attractive as possible. People will be coming to the wedding from various parts of your locality and this will be a wonderful way for you to attract people who aren't normally your customers.

9 Once you get a good, cooperative group of merchants together, you'll all start stimulating one another with promotional, publicity, and public relations ideas. All the merchants will have signs on their premises advertising the bridal show, and over the course of weeks, with everyone's customers seeing the signs and telling all the brides they know, you will miss absolutely no one. Every bridal party will show up. Just to be on the safe side, though, you'll want to run some advertising in local newspapers.

Once you do a bridal show for the first time, you and all the other merchants will want to do one every year. Every year they'll get better and better. You may even get to the point where you actually hire someone whose sole responsibility for a few months will be to conceptualize, coordinate, and produce the show for you. You'll have to pay a fee, of course, but, again, when you divide it among all the merchants, and when you realize how much business the activity brings in, you may find the coordinator's fee is well worth it.

Networking

Capture Neighborhood Store Owners' and Employees' Business

NETWORKING

The vast proportion of salons are located in neighborhood shopping areas, malls, and strip malls. If you are one of these, you have dozens, perhaps hundreds, of potential clients right in your immediate vicinity. Every store and shop owner and every employee of these stores and shops comes in daily contact with the public, and each of them is conscious of their need to look their very best. All of them need salon services, but how many are your clients? We want to convert them into clients, and here's a beautiful way to do it.

1 There's a general friendliness among store and shop owners (unless, of course, they're arch competitors) and a loose feeling that they're all in the same "club." It's fairly easy to build up a mailing list of all these "club" members. All you have to do is walk around the neighborhood, the shopping center, or mall you're targeting. Write down the name and address of each establishment. You're going to send each of them a personal letter. Even more preferable is visiting them personally. It might take a few weeks to complete the task, but your upcoming promotion will be more successful as a result.

2 The promotion? On a one-time basis, offer owners and *employees* of all these neighborhood shops and stores any service they'd like to have, absolutely FREE—*providing* that the service will be performed on an early-in-the-week slow day when your stylists have ample down time.

3 Obviously the offer is all but irresistible. Who could resist a free haircut, haircolor, perm, or conditioning? And why would anybody want to resist?

4 The benefits accruing to your salon from these free appointments can be enormous. First of all, it's likely that better than half of these people will sign up for future appointments at *regular* prices. If you'd like to take the promotion one step further, offer them discounts on all future appointments as long as they are in business in the neighborhood. The discount percentages are up to you.

5 Remember, too, that in addition to the business represented by these new clients you'll get yet another major advantage: They'll all be displaying the kind of work done in your salon, and they'll be displaying it right there in your neighborhood. We all know that word of mouth is the best kind of advertising there is. As thousands of people pass through the stores and shops in the targeted area, they'll be looking at and chatting with *your* customers. If your salon turns out the kind of work that makes people ask, "Who did your hair?" you'll soon have hundreds of referrals.

6 As a special "plus" for these special clients, you can tell each of them when they're in the salon that you understand they're always under some sort of time pressure. Tell them you'll give them preferred treatment in terms of "squeezing them in" and making special appointments. Let them know, too, that everyone in the salon will be tuned in to getting them in and out as quickly as possible. They'll appreciate this warm neighborliness, and you'll lock in an unusually loyal clientele.

7 Finally, all the products you use and time expended giving away free services are tax deductible. Keep accurate records, and clue your accountant in to what you're doing.

Coaches Can Be Great Business Builders

NETWORKING

PLAN A PROMOTION
THAT WILL ATTRACT
YOUNG STAR
ATHLETES—BOYS
AS WELL AS GIRLS.

We all know the adulation athletes get. From Babe Ruth to Michael Jordan, and thousands of athletes in between, we read about them, we follow them, we follow their careers, we pay to see them play, and if it were possible, we'd love to meet them. It's not just the high-profile pros on TV that our society adores. It's all athletes. Right now, in your neighborhood, there are athletes who are put on a pedestal by a whole segment of the population. The segment? High school kids. The athletes? Anyone who's on any of the high school teams. If you could attract a good portion of some of these teams, it would, like a magic magnet, attract scores of their peers. So plan a promotion that will attract young star athletes—boys as well as girls.

1 The best way to get to the teams is through their coaches. The coaches are approachable. They live in the vicinity; they are your neighbors; you see them in the supermarkets. Start by scheduling an appointment with one of them. Your approach will be that you are a booster of the high school and of the team. You know that team members are looked up to by the rest of the student population and should, therefore, be role models. They should be role models not only in their athleticism and sportsmanship but in their appearance, as well. If they are unkempt, disheveled, and poorly groomed, that sends the wrong message of what an athlete should look like. What, indeed, *should* an athlete look like? The answer is any way they want to look—but within the boundaries of being clean, reasonably neat, and decently groomed.

2 You'll find as you discuss this that the coach will probably be nodding his head as you go along. He doesn't want any of his kids to look like wild people or goons. Invite the coach to visit your salon for a haircut and any other appropriate services, with your compliments. Tell him that if he approves of the atmosphere in your salon and the way it operates, you'd like to offer the kids on his team special discounts during the entire season that the particular sport is played. The discount is up to you. Kids generally have spendable income, but they may not choose to spend it in a salon. So the discount will probably have to be formidable to make it attractive. Maybe as high as 50 percent.

3 For the moment let's assume it's the football team. That's a lot of haircuts at half price. But if you arrange the promotion so that their appointments can only be made when you're slow, it will help fill empty slots, and you'll be attracting business that will attract even more business. You must assure the coach that you won't do anything he disapproves of. If there's any particular kind of cut or style the coach frowns on, you simply won't do it. At the same time, the player's must be assured that they're going to get the kind of cuts they want. They're not going to be subjected to crew cuts—unless they want them.

4 If the coach is amenable to the idea, your work is just starting. For their first visit, ask if you can have all the kids on the team into the salon on the same day and all at the same time. Make it a Sunday or a Monday when there won't be other clients. When the team and the coach arrive, make sure you have a photographer handy. Have some photos taken of the whole process. The school may be willing to post the photos, and if so, so much the better. Have plenty of soft drinks and munchies around so that no one gets restless and leaves. When everybody is done, have them all line up for a team photo—but this will be a photo that includes *your* team as well as theirs. All in all, the day's activities should be a lot of fun for everyone.

5 Before this event takes place, call the sports editor and/or the society editor of your local newspaper, and tell them about the activity that's going to take place. Ask if they'd like to cover it and maybe get a fun story out of it. If they do write it up, or print any photos, you will absolutely be the talk of the town.

6 Whether or not you get newspaper coverage, make a big blowup of the team photo, and post it prominently in your window at the start of the season, or before a big game. That alone will cause a lot of buzz. Invariably the high school has some sort of newspaper, and they're always soliciting ads. They don't cost much, and usually they don't do a heck of a lot of good except for some goodwill. But if you take an ad, publish the team pictures with copy that reads something like: GOOD LUCK TO THE CENTRAL WARRIORS FROM THE TEAM AT NEW IMAGE SALON. It will attract attention; it will bring in business.

You can be sure that during the days following the time when the whole team came in, there will be a lot of talk at the school. The talk will be kidding, but the talk will be about appearance. And if you've done your job well and everyone on the team likes the way they look, you'll attract friends,

YOU CAN BE SURE THAT THERE WILL BE A LOT OF TALK AT THE SCHOOL ABOUT APPEARANCE.

relatives, teachers, and other students. That is, after all, what we set out to do at the start, isn't it?

Remember, all of this was just for one team. You can do it for as many teams as you'd like. And always remember that it won't be very long before these boys and girls will be men and women in the work force. Their good times in your salon will pay off for years to come.

NOTES

Work with Real Estate Agents

NETWORKING

We are a country on the move. To convince yourself of this, simply take a look at the pages and pages of homes for sale in the real estate section of the newspapers. And look at all those For Sale signs right around your own neighborhood. Check the number of real estate offices in your town. There'll be a lot, and many offices have a dozen or more agents working out of them. These agents see thousands of people in the course of a year, all of whom are looking to buy property or homes not too far from the location of your salon. In the initial search for a new home, more often than not it's the woman of the house who goes out with the real estate agent. Bingo! What an opportunity for referrals

A REAL ESTATE AGENT

IS AN OPPORTUNITY

FOR REFERRALS.

1 Start off small. Find a relative, friend, or friend of a friend who's an active real estate agent. Take her out to lunch. Invite her into your salon. Offer to cut and style her hair at no charge; then offer a 25 percent discount on all her future visits. Explain that your generosity does not come with strings attached or obligations on her part—but if any of the women she shows houses to comments about how pretty her hair is or asks if she "knows a good salon in this neighborhood," you'd appreciate a referral.

2 Tell this real estate agent that if she would like to recommend another associate or two in her office, you'll be happy to offer them the same courtesy.

3 Even though you will have told two or three women that they are "under no obligation," you can be assured that they'll be grateful and will try to help whenever they can. You *will* get referrals. They won't be knocking down your doors in numbers, but they will come. Remember, each one represents a potential of hundreds of dollars a year in services and products.

4 Once you feel comfortable with the program and see that you are getting referrals, expand. Make the offer available to all the women in that real estate office. You can even include the men. They see hundreds of

people, too. Their clients may not effusively compliment their hairstyles, but the men can definitely have opportunities to steer people in your direction.

5 If after six months or so you're satisfied that you're receiving a decent amount of referrals, you can expand to yet another real estate office. Chances are even before you decide to expand, some of the agents in other offices will have heard about your program and will come in asking if they can participate. Whether or not you expand and how fast is up to you. This is a very economical kind of promotion. No signs, no advertising, no printing, no mailing costs, no out-of-pocket layouts at all. Your only cost is the discounts these folks will be getting. And see your accountant: The discounts and freebies may be deductible as advertising expenses.

We all know that walking advertisements in the form of beautiful hair is the best advertising there is. Real estate people know that they must make good visual impressions. If they were simply walking down the street or sitting in a restaurant, women who admired their hair might be a bit reluctant to approach them about it. But when they have the close relationships that real estate agents have with their clients, they positively will be talking about where to eat, where to shop, and where to get their hair and nails done. "I go to this wonderful little salon right here in town." That's what they'll be saying, and your no-outlay "investment" will pay off handsomely.

YOUR NO-OUTLAY
"INVESTMENT" WILL
PAY OFF HANDSOMELY.

Lecture/Demos:
A Sure Thing

NETWORKING

PROGRAM

CHAIRPERSONS

ARE ALWAYS

SCOUTING FOR

ATTENDANCE-BUILDING

ATTRACTIONS.

There is no part of the country that doesn't have an abundance of social organizations: garden clubs, women's investment clubs, church and synagogue groups, American Legion auxiliaries, career women's groups, and so on. One thing all of these groups have in common is that they all have a program chairperson, the person who plans the programs to make the meetings interesting. Being program chairperson is a tough job. If the next meeting's program sounds interesting, attendance will be high. If it sounds dull, attendance will be sparse. So you may take for granted that program chairpersons are always scouting for attendance-building attractions. You and/or members of your staff can be the answer to every chairperson's prayer. Regardless of the nature or mission of each organization, if it's primarily made up of women, they'll be interested in having a lecture demonstration on one aspect of beauty or another. Speaking to a group of five or fifty women about an aspect of beauty that's of particular interest to them is just about the perfect way to make five or fifty new friends.

Consider:

- You'll be standing up, they'll be sitting down—automatically a psychologically superior position for you.

- You're the teacher, they're the students—automatically they'll have faith in what you say.

- They'll *always* have questions, insecurities, and vulnerabilities in specific areas—you'll always have answers and expertise.

- Because of the above, they will be putty in your hands—*provided* you are well prepared.

Here are some checkpoints you'll have to cover and consider to maximize the results of your lecture/demonstrations:

1 Of paramount importance is the enhancement and refinement of your presentation skills. The worst thing you can do in speaking before a group is to bomb because you're a poor presenter. But remember, good presenters aren't born, they're made. You can take courses that will make you a

really effective speaker. (The Dale Carnegie courses are excellent.) Most community colleges have courses in public speaking. There are dozens of books on the subject. Read the books, take the courses.

2 Practice, practice, practice—but not silently. Go into a room, close the door, and emote. Got a video camera? Tape yourself; then watch the tapes. You may cringe at the beginning, but as you practice, practice, practice, you'll improve, improve, improve.

3 When you think you're ready, assemble a small audience of some friends or relatives or members of your staff. Do your thing and ask them to critique it.

4 Now you're ready to "open." Research local newspapers and yellow pages. Network among friends and clients. You're looking for appropriate groups who'll be interested in a competent, professional demonstration on one of the many aspects of cosmetology. You could speak on the perils and pleasures of haircoloring and/or perms. You can discuss the psychological aspects of beauty in terms of feeling better when you're looking better in the mirror. You can discuss the art of makeup, shade selection, and cosmetic products. You can talk about the joys and benefits of skin care or waxing or nail art. The potential subjects are limitless. What do you like best? What is your greatest area of expertise? Your first lectures should always be on what you know and like most.

YOUR FIRST LECTURES SHOULD ALWAYS BE ON WHAT YOU KNOW AND LIKE MOST.

5 When you have the names of appropriate organizations, find out who the program chairpersons are, and then contact them, telling each of them what you're prepared to do.

6 Don't overbook at the beginning. When you've got one lecture/demo under your belt, step back, take a deep breath, and see how you can make improvements. When you feel you really have your act together, you can book a little more expansively.

7 Your program should consist of a relatively small introduction before going right into the demonstration. Don't do it alone. Have members of your staff assist you both on and off the platform. If any of your staff are particularly good at communicating, share the platform. That way when one is talking, the other is working and vice versa.

8 Always have a model to work on at the start. Ask the program chairperson for her recommendations as to which members of the organization may be interested in volunteering.

9 Check with the program chairperson regarding the most effective lecture length for her membership. Always keep it on the relatively shorter side rather than the relatively longer side.

10 Make sure you leave plenty of time for questions and answers. There will *always* be questions. But don't let the Q & A period drag on too long. You must develop a sense of it. After a time people get restless because the questions can go on forever, and they don't know when they're going to get out of there. At a certain point say you'll take two more questions, and then end the program.

11 When the lecture is over, be enthusiastic in expressing appreciation to the organization. *Make absolutely certain to give your calling cards to everybody in the room.* Announce that you will be happy to offer a 10 percent discount to all members of the organization on their first appointment.

It's impossible to overestimate the importance of presentation skills. You'll find that when your platform skills are such that the audience pays attention when you want them to pay attention, laughs when you want them to laugh, asks questions when you want them to ask questions, and start getting repeat invitations from the same organizations and getting new invitations from people who have heard about your lectures, at that point you will probably be able to abandon all other promotions and promotional devices. You'll be able to get all the new clients you can accommodate. You'll be in demand and will be able to enjoy the benefits of the Law of Supply and Demand. The greater the *demand* for your lecture/demos the greater the *supply* of new clients—and won't that be great?

Rebates to Women's Organizations

NETWORKING

You've no doubt participated in this type of promotion yourself at one time or other. You buy a product or service, and you're told a certain percentage of your purchase goes to some charitable organization or other. Every town, city, and hamlet in the country has several women's organizations. We are a country of joiners and probably every one of your clients belongs to not one but several clubs, organizations, or groups.

One thing that every one of these organizations has in common is they all need money. They're always fundraising. You can tie in to this never-ending need for funds by turning it all into a never-ending promotion. Here's how.

1 Target these local groups, and schedule an appointment with their presidents. Your offer is that whenever a member of any specific organization visits your salon, she will receive a receipt for the total amount of her expenditure. She turns in the receipt to the club's treasurer, who accumulates them. Once a month, once a quarter, or once a year, these receipts are totaled, and you rebate a percentage to the club.

2 This is "found money" for the club. All they have to do on their part is inform their members (hopefully at every meeting and in their mailings) that these rebates are available to the club whenever members patronize *your* salon. That's pretty good publicity. These notifications alone will be good publicity for your salon.

3 Then, too, you should ask for a list of the mailing addresses of all members in the group. In this way you could send periodic reminders of the good deed members will be doing when they have all of their beauty services performed in your salon.

4 Another lovely plus to this promotion is that you can attract women who are new to the community. Very often when a woman relocates, she will hasten to join a community organization in which she's interested, and her primary motive may be simply to meet and make new friends. And she'll certainly want to know what beauty salon her new friends

TIE IN TO THE NEVER-ENDING NEED FOR FUNDS BY TURNING IT INTO A NEVER-ENDING PROMOTION.

recommend. Ta-da—they'll recommend *you* because of your rebate program.

On top of all this, check with your accountant. All your rebates can probably be considered "advertising" and are therefore deductible.

A final advantage of this program is that because you are a benefactor of the organization, you'll probably be excused from the incessant donations, raffles, and various other appeals these organizations invariably have going.

You're a friend of the community; you're a friend of womens' organizations; people talk about you; people recommend your salon. You can't ask for too much more than that.

Benefit from Other Merchants' Cooperation

NETWORKING

Next time you go to a department store, notice how they cross-merchandise their various departments. If they have fashion mannequins arranged around a piece of furniture, they'll note the piece is available on another floor in their furniture department. If any fashion display contains sporting equipment they'll direct you where in the store to find that equipment. Very often their beauty salon is in a remote part of the store, and there are signs in the elevators and various departments, telling customer where it is. You can use this principle even though your salon's not in a department store. Let's go one step at a time.

1. In the aggregate, your neighborhood merchants constitute a complete department store. If you approach them right, they'll probably be willing to help you.

2. Is there a dress shop or two in your immediate vicinity? How about providing wigs for the mannequins in their window displays in exchange for a sign saying that the wigs are available at your salon?

3. Did you know that the makeup on mannequins in most department stores is often real makeup? You can offer your makeup services for the mannequins in your neighborhood dress shops, again in exchange for a sign giving you appropriate credit.

4. How about a sign at the local photographer's? It can suggest a professional makeup and hairstyle refresher immediately before a photography sitting. If the photographer is amenable to one of these signs, what does he get in return? Any salon service you'd care to make available to him or his wife on a complimentary basis.

5. You'd be amazed what you can get for a free shampoo and blowout. Want to sweeten the offer? Throw in a haircut. Obviously, when you make these barter deals, you'd only book the cooperating merchant during slow hours.

USE THE CROSS-MERCHANDISE PRINCIPLE, EVEN THOUGH YOUR SALON'S NOT IN A DEPARTMENT STORE.

NOTES

6 I know a salon that has a reciprocity arrangement with the local movie house. A poster noting the current program at the cinema is always in the salon's window. Once a month all the kids (and the manager) working at the movie come in for a free salon hair service. The salon also supplies these folks with a T-shirt that says "MY HAIR WAS DONE AT THE MARGARET STUDIO ON MAIN STREET." They wear this T-shirt to work on one specific day of the month, and of course, several hundred people see these walking advertisements every month. (As a bonus, the salon owner and her husband are always admitted to the movie on a complimentary basis.)

7 Bridal shops can be gold mines for business. You should have complete bridal specials available through these bridal shops. Always make sure to leave plenty of calling cards at these shops. In return you can periodically put a sign in your own window, advertising that particular bridal shop.

8 Walk down the street with one or two of your favorite stylists. As you pass each local merchant, stop and brainstorm with one another about how that particular store or shop could help you and what you could do in return for them.

A sign appearing in several local store windows, plus having several merchants and employees recommending your salon because they go there themselves, can be absolute magic. The old saying "One hand washes the other" rings true when it comes to mutual cooperation with local merchants.

Promotional Opportunities from Your Local Newspaper

NETWORKING

One of the ways that publishers and editors of local newspapers get their readership is to cover every conceivable social event in the community. They want to know everything that is going on, and they want to put a notice about events in the paper. People are trained to read the paper to find out what's going on, and this increases the circulation base. How can you take advantage of all this?

1. What you have to do is go through the newspaper with a fine-tooth comb. Note all the events that are scheduled to take place—events like dances, theater parties, card parties, golf tournaments, and so on. The chairpersons of each of these events do everything they can to make them more enjoyable and attractive. One of the best ways is to make prizes available to attendees. Once they come upon the idea of giving out prizes, they then have to go out and beg local merchants to donate things.

2. Turn the tables on them. Instead of them coming to you to beg, you go to them to offer. Volunteer various of your salon's services as prizes. Depending on whom you want to attract, the prizes can be for men, women, or children. Maybe you're eager to promote a special new service in your salon. Perhaps skin care, perhaps nail care. Offer that service as your prize.

VOLUNTEER VARIOUS OF YOUR SALON'S SERVICES AS PRIZES.

3. As you go through the newspapers day after day, you'll find more opportunities to donate prizes than you really care to. Pick and choose the types of organizations you want to work with. They invariably have a person's name and/or phone number connected with the newspaper announcement, so call that person. They'll be delighted to hear from you.

4. Tell the chairperson that donating the prize is really a form of advertising for you, and you would appreciate getting recognition at the organization's meetings or in their newsletters or announcements.

It won't be too long before chairpersons of just about all the local organizations hear about you and learn about your willingness to donate prizes. Then they'll come knocking at your door. Be as generous or as conservative as you'd care to.

Over the course of time you'll engender an enormous amount of goodwill. Activists in the community, the people who join organizations, the people who attend meetings will all hear about you. The prize winners will be grateful to you and will talk about you. It will build and build, and over the course of months you'll have a significant number of clients whose patronage will be directly traceable to winning prizes.

5 If you want to jump-start this activity as you slowly feel your way in reading about social activities, speak to your clients one at a time over the course of some weeks. You don't have to hit everyone, just as many as you can. Tell them you appreciate their loyalty, and to show your appreciation, you'd like to donate a prize to any organization they may be affiliated with. Clients can't help but appreciate your kindness, and whether or not they belong to any organizations, they'll feel warmly toward you for having asked.

Adapt a Department Store Promotion for Yourself

NETWORKING

Department stores are masters of cross-merchandising. Various departments give plugs to one another. Displays give credit for some of the items that come from other departments. Elevators have signs directing you to special areas.

A very frequent department store promotion is the fashion show. They've got their list of customers in their computer, and whenever they have anything exciting to show in fashion (a new line, cruise wear, evening attire, seasonal fashions), they invite their customers to call in and make reservations for these private fashion shows. Women love to attend. They see a fashion event, they stay up-to-date on what's happening in the world of fashion, and there is no pressure or obligation to buy.

Obviously, department stores run these fashion shows to sell fashion merchandise. But they want to do more. They'd also like to bring in some business to their beauty salon. So they ask the salon to do the cuts and hairstyles on all the runway models. Sometime during the show they will make it a special point to call attention to the fact that "all these gorgeous hairstyles were done right here in our own beauty salon on the fifth floor." Then they'll often introduce the manager of the salon, or they'll have the stylists come out from backstage to take a bow. Often, too, they'll tell the women in attendance that "just for today, and just for the women in this room, there will be a twenty-five percent discount on appointments booked today for any services performed during the next thirty days."

It's a soft sell. It doesn't get in the way of the main fashion presentation. It gets the point across. And it brings in business. It works for department stores, and will work for you.

1 Contact one of the fashion stores close to your salon. You may not even be aware that these stores do fashion shows and have been doing them for years. They concentrate on putting across the fashions and accessories and often leave the makeup and hair to the models themselves. If you offer your salon's services, they will instantly see the advantages that you'll bring to their presentations. Your help with hair and makeup will make each model more beautiful, more dramatic looking.

2 Consult with the shop owners to determine what kinds of hairstyles they'd like to see. Dramatic? Casual? Avant-garde? Wash 'n wear? This consultation takes place at every major fashion presentation, with every major couturier in the world. The fashion designer sits down with the hair designer to determine what would look best to make the most effective presentation. That's exactly what you'll do with the dress-shop owner.

3 The whole exercise is wonderful training, too. Doing your regular clientele month in, month out, year in, year out can sometimes get you into a self-satisfied rut. It's good for all artists to challenge themselves now and again, and these fashion presentations will present these challenges. You and your staff will have to stretch a bit, and that's creatively healthy.

4 Of course, you'll have a complete understanding with the fashion-shop owner that your salon will be given appropriate credit in her commentary, and you and your stylists will be asked to appear on stage for a quick bow somewhere during the course of the proceedings.

5 You should also come to some sort of understanding as to how people in the audience can be directed to schedule appointments at your salon and under whatever discount arrangements you care to make. The fashion-store owner may not want you to put a business card on each individual chair to pass through the audience distributing these cards. Perhaps she'll be giving away some trinket or piece of literature; your card could certainly ride along with that. Or there could be a stack of cards left on a table so that everyone who wanted one could take one. Or the shop owner could provide you with a list of names and addresses of everyone in the audience, and you could send them a card within a day or two, saying what a pleasure it was to create the hairstyles at the fashion show and make so many new friends. You can then offer these friends whatever inducement you'd like for them to come by and get acquainted.

Once you do one or two of these and the word gets around, you'll probably be contacted by other fashion-shop owners, asking if you'd be willing to do the same for them. The more you do, the more your salon's reputation will be enhanced and broadened.

One of the nice things about these kinds of promotions is that you won't have to write any checks. The cost is minimal in terms of out-of-pocket outlay. You don't have to print anything or advertise anything or mail anything. Yes, you have to devote time. But it is time that will enhance the skills and reputations of everyone in the salon.

"Wish You Were Here" Can Pay Off

NETWORKING

Do you have a beautiful salon, outside or inside? If your salon is attractive enough on the outside that you are proud of it and think its appearance will attract some clients, or if you've just remodeled and you feel that if folks could see how beautiful the whole setup is that they'd probably want to be there, you've got a potential promotion in the making. Hire a local photographer to take professional color photos of the salon. Choose the one you think is most appealing. Conceivably you may choose the best outside shot *and* the best inside shot. Then go to a printer and have postcards printed up.

There are many postcard promotions in this book, so you'll have lots of potential use for the postcards. If you have two different views that you're proud of, have two sets of cards printed. The very first mailing you do should be to nonclients. There's not a lot of room to write on the back of a picture postcard, so you'll have to keep it short. This will surely do.

WISH YOU WERE HERE!
Our salon is beautiful, our hairstylists are tops,
our colorists are experts, our nail artists are artistic,
our prices are moderate. Call for an appointment.

With this message and this supply of postcards you should always be on the lookout and on the alert for new people moving into the neighborhood. Some major sources for scouting them out would be:

1 Your local pharmacists. Families moving to a new neighborhood have to have their prescriptions filled in a new drugstore. If you're in a strip-mall salon, chances are the druggist will be one of your neighbors. Ask for his cooperation in exchange for some free services.

2 Your clients. They know instantly when somebody new moves in next door or across the street. If they report a new arrival who's not already on your mailing list, give them a retail product that you got a good buy on. If that referral converts to being a client, the cost of the product you gave away will be a piddling amount to pay.

ALWAYS BE ON THE LOOKOUT AND ON THE ALERT FOR NEW PEOPLE MOVING INTO THE NEIGHBORHOOD.

NOTES

Welcome Wagon lady. If you have one of these in your area, just know that she makes her living by scouting out new people in town. Of course, she'll want to recruit you as one of her own clients to talk about when she visits new arrivals. This may not be a bad idea for you, and you may want to consider it. If not, try to work a barter deal with her. Her appearance is paramount, so she probably spends a fair amount of money on cosmetics and hair care. Offer her a discount for every name she gives you. If she supplies you with enough referrals, she'll wind up getting free beauty services, and you'll wind up with a heck of a new mailing list.

These WISH YOU WERE HERE cards can also be effective in inviting clients to come in who haven't made an appointment in a while. You'll have to have a special message for them, and you should give them an extra incentive to come in again. Tell them to bring the card with them, and they'll automatically receive either a generous discount, a free service, or a free hair care product. Obviously you won't get them all back, but if you just get a few, it will pay for all your printing costs and then some.

Cards with photos of your salon are versatile. You can do small mailings, large mailings, holiday mailings, discount mailings, and on and on. And in each one the photo itself will be saying, "We're very proud of our salon."

There's No Business Like Show Business

NETWORKING

Do you ever wait in the movies after the picture is done and they scroll through the screen credits? Or when you go to the theater, do you ever thumb through the *Playbill, Stagebill,* or whatever the show program is called? When you come to the person who gets credit for the hairstyling, wigs, or makeup, don't you have a little special respect for that person's expertise?

You're in the business, and you *still* have that extra measure of respect. What if you're not in the business? You're just a regular person, and you read through the credits, and you know that the people who worked on the motion picture or the play or the production have a special kind of expertise, a special kind of talent. It automatically follows that they are accorded a special kind of respect. You and your salon—large or small, in any location in the country, big city, suburban, or rural—can earn that same kind of extra measure of respect. Absolutely.

In every locality, in every nook and cranny of the country, there are theater groups—community theater, amateur theater, ladies' club theater, fraternity club theater. Everybody is always putting on plays, programs, skits, and productions, and everybody needs professional help with hair and makeup. Most theater groups don't have professional help so they do it themselves—and nobody gets the credit. *You* could be getting the credit. And when you do get that credit, it means that hundreds of people will be seeing your name and your salon name in the program credits. Hundreds of people will be exposed to your name and your talents. And it costs you absolutely nothing out-of-pocket. Here's what you do.

EVERYBODY IS ALWAYS PUTTING ON PLAYS AND PRODUCTIONS, AND EVERYBODY NEEDS PROFESSIONAL HELP WITH HAIR AND MAKEUP.

1 Scour your local newspapers for advance information on any sort of theatrical program any group is scheduling, and contact the person in charge. Or if you know of any permanent amateur theater groups, do the same, and get in touch with the head of the theater company.

2 Tell him/her that you'd like to volunteer your and your salon's professional hair and makeup services for their productions. They will be overjoyed and welcome you with open arms.

NOTES

3 As a condition for your valuable services, tell them you require only a couple of things: a) They'll need to give your salon credit for hair and makeup work, these credits to include your address and phone number. b) A small complimentary ad in the advertising section of the program, again giving your name, address, and phone number. These are reasonable requests and should pose no difficulty at all.

4 If possible, ask that members of the cast come to your salon for some of the rehearsal preparation work. This may not be possible, but to the extent that you can attract some cast members into your salon, it will be a plus.

5 Stretch your talents. Do a bit of research so that the makeup and hairstyles you execute are reasonably authentic for the period of the play or revue. That's a fun exercise, and you'll no doubt find plenty of pictorial material in your local library.

6 Don't do it alone. Involve members of your staff—but strictly on a voluntary basis. The ones who volunteer will be the ones who want to associate themselves with show business. They will be eager and do the extra work without grumbling.

7 Get friendly with the entire company. Once they see you cutting hair, styling wigs, shaping beards, applying makeup, one by one they'll come to you for "counseling" about their own personal grooming problems. It goes without saying that just about everyone who comes to you as a "patient" will evolve into a client.

8 Sometimes on opening night or closing night everyone who's had anything to do with the production is brought out. Make sure you're included for a bow. You can never tell who in the audience will have been impressed with your work and will want to seek you out for your services.

9 During the course of the production and/or the rehearsal period, take pictures, pictures, pictures. If anyone is doing publicity for the production, ask them to send one of your pictures along with a little blurb to local newspapers. If no one is in charge of publicity, send pictures yourself, and write the blurb yourself. It doesn't have to be deathless prose. If it's interesting local news, the editors will rewrite and rephrase the story in their own styles. When you send out any publicity photos, make sure they are 8 × 10s, not little snapshots. Photos needn't be in color; black and white will usually do and is usually preferred.

10 Put some of these photos in your window and/or inside the salon along with an appropriate sign that announces that you're doing the hair and makeup for this upcoming production.

When it's all over and the production has closed, it will have been a very positive experience. You will have gained a lot of new friends, many of whom will become clients. Your salon will have been exposed to hundreds of people, and new clients are certain to come out of this pool, as well. You will have expanded your creativity into areas where you normally wouldn't have ventured. And finally, you will have had lots of fun. Hey, what a combination. Who could ask for anything more?

WHEN THE PRODUCTION IS OVER, YOU'LL HAVE GAINED A LOT OF NEW FRIENDS—AND HAD LOTS OF FUN.

Early-Bird Hours for Local Merchants

NETWORKING

CAPTURE FRUSTRATED

MERCHANTS AND

EMPLOYEES BY

MAKING SPECIAL

HOURS FOR THEM.

Most stores in shopping centers, strip malls and local neighborhoods open at 9 A.M. They close at varying hours, usually between 6 P.M. and 9 P.M. and they are usually open six days a week, sometimes seven. What do the owners of these stores and their employees do about beauty services? Yes, they can run in during a lunch hour for a quick cut or a quickie color service, but it's a rushed, frantic, harried experience. The other alternative is, of course, to have their beauty services done on their day off. Chances are most of them do take this precious time for their salon appointments. And which salon are they going to? Is it yours? Why not capture all of these frustrated merchants and employees by making special hours for them?

If 9:00 is the general opening time, open your salon at 8:00 or even 7:30, and let them know about it. Your marketing/promotional plan should go something like this:

1 Arrange a meeting with your entire staff. Explain what you are trying to do, and find out which of your employees is willing to come in early and on which days. You may be surprised at how many volunteer. Starting the day earlier can either mean ending it earlier, enabling some to finish up in time to pick up their kids or prepare dinner. Or they may simply look at it as an opportunity to make more money, both in commissions and tips.

2 Personally visit as many merchants as you can. Explain what you're trying to do. Get a feel for what types of services they and their employees would be interested in. Get a feel for what days would be most popular.

3 Have cards printed that say something like:

SPECIAL COURTESY HOURS
EXCLUSIVELY FOR LOCAL MERCHANTS AND THEIR EMPLOYEES

Sylvia's Beauty Salon, 123 Main Street, Elmsford
will be opening its doors an hour earlier (8 A.M.)
exclusively to serve the beauty needs of local merchants and
their employees.
During these early-bird hours we will also extend a
professional discount
on all services and products.
By appointment only. Please call 987–6543.

When you visit the local merchants, regardless of whether they have great or little interest, ask them, "May I leave these courtesy cards for you and your employees?"

4 Print a letter on your stationery explaining and reiterating your new policy. That means they will have heard it from you personally, be reminded by the cards you leave behind, and be reminded yet again by your letter.

5 Make sure you schedule yourself to come in during all the early hours. You'll want to greet your neighbors, the local merchants, and their employees personally, and you'll want to see exactly how it's all working out schedule-wise so that you can make appropriate changes where necessary.

6 Don't book too tightly. Remember, these clients are coming in a rush. They positively can't be kept waiting. Make sure you leave enough time for whatever services they are booked for.

7 Don't be impatient. This is a new policy for you, and it's even newer for them. They're going to other salons now, and they won't immediately switch. They have other time and scheduling habits, and these take a while to change. Word of mouth is going to do most of the building, and this takes time. Give it a few months.

When you get, say, half a dozen favorable reactions, ask if you can quote these reactions and name the people and the businesses they work in. Incorporate these into yet another letter that will go out to local merchants two months after your policy is in effect.

SOME LOCAL MERCHANTS WILL EXTEND RECIPROCAL DISCOUNTS TO YOU AND YOUR EMPLOYEES.

A by-product of your early-bird hours and your courtesy discounts will be an enhanced personal and commercial relationship with these local merchants. You'll find that, in return, some of them will extend special reciprocal courtesy discounts to your employees. Your own employees will love that.

And finally, this policy means that when you open your doors for your regular customers at your regular hours, you'll already have a decent amount of cash in the register. Won't that be nice?

Beauty Salon As Art Gallery and Vice Versa

NETWORKING

MAKE YOUR SALON
INTO AN ART GALLERY.
IT'S EASIER THAN
YOU THINK.

You and I know—and everyone who's a hairstylist knows—that a lot of artistry is executed in the beauty salon. Outsiders may think it's technical or mechanical or even scientific. Insiders know it is all these things *plus* the artistry that's in the hands and the heart of the cosmetologist. One way to convey that the salon is a place where art lives is to transform it into a place where art is not only practiced on hair but displayed on the walls. In other words, make your salon into an art gallery. It's easier than you think and will be more fun than you can imagine. Let's lay it out.

1 Take stock of your interior walls. Depending on the size, you may be able to hang maybe a dozen pieces of art or photography. If you have anywhere near this kind of space, go to the next step.

2 Check in your immediate local community. Chances are very likely that there's an art club or artist's group of some sort that meets on a regular basis just to talk about art and to help one another. They may not have headquarters, they may not have a specific phone number, but they exist. You'll just have to ferret them out.

3 Meet with this group and tell them that you have space you're willing to devote to an exhibit of their work. They will welcome you with open arms.

4 Invite them over to your salon so that they can see your space and make suggestions as to what would be appropriate to hang where. They no doubt will be very cooperative in working with you and in actually mounting the various pieces of art.

5 Schedule each exhibit to last anywhere between a month and two. Ask the art group to do all the publicity work. They can contact the art editors of local newspapers and send out mailings to their friends. They'll probably even suggest that there be a gala champagne opening—for which they will pick up the tab.

6 Remember, too, that even though hanging art enhances the overall image of your salon, you won't be offering space simply for free. Each of the pieces of art will have a price on it, and if any are sold during the exhibit period, you'll be entitled to a commission, which can range anywhere from 15 to 20 percent of the selling price.

7 When a particular exhibit is over, that isn't the end of your gallery experience. All the while you should be scouting about and inquiring among friends and clients for other artists and photographers who would be interested and eager to have their work exhibited for a month or two. When one exhibit is over, let a few weeks go by, and then mount another. This means another set of people to contact local editors, another opening party, another group of people to come and see artwork.

8 During the course of all this activity you'll be meeting a whole new population. Most of the artists and photographers will probably become clients. You'll be exposed to their admirers, relatives, and friends, many of whom may also become clients. And finally, your salon will be looked upon as a place where art is practiced and exhibited, and this alone will attract new clients.

Just consider for a moment that this whole exercise is one that will garner an ongoing series of events in your salon, an ongoing series of publicity blurbs in local newspapers, an ongoing succession of people coming in who would normally not be visiting your salon, and an ongoing income from commission on sold artwork. That's lots of pluses. The minuses are that you'll have to come in on an occasional Sunday or Monday when the exhibits are being mounted, and you'll wind up with a few nail holes in your walls. Pretty small price to pay for all the extra business you'll do and fun you'll have, as well as your new status as a "patron of the arts."

YOUR SALON WILL BE LOOKED UPON AS A PLACE WHERE ART IS PRACTICED AND EXHIBITED, AND THIS ALONE WILL ATTRACT NEW CLIENTS.

Go after Corporate Business

NETWORKING

It used to be that offices were located "downtown." No longer. Corporations discovered the suburbs years ago, and now we see office buildings, corporate parks and industrial parks out in the suburbs, where folks live. If you're located anywhere within a five-minute drive of an office complex, just know that there are dozens, perhaps hundreds, of potential clients waiting for you to "ask for the order," or "make them an offer they can't refuse." All these folks, men and women, may be driving, or walking, right by your salon on the way to and from their jobs. Let's reach out to them.

1 First, always start out with your own clientele. You may know their names, addresses, and phone numbers, but do you know where they're employed? If you don't, start finding out by asking them to fill out cards indicating the place where they are employed, the address, and the phone number. Be open about it. Tell them you're trying to formulate a plan to attract more clients from local companies.

2 If you find that, coincidentally, several of your clients are employed at the same company or at the same location, ask them who in that company you can contact to present a plan to make it attractive for their employees to patronize your salon.

3 At the same time, if you know of companies that are nearby, attempt to make contact with the human resources manager or the boss. Write and explain that you want to offer special incentives to their employees who come into the salon for services. Your letter should state that you will call for an appointment within the next few days.

PRESENT A PLAN TO MAKE IT ATTRACTIVE FOR A COMPANY'S EMPLOYEES TO PATRONIZE YOUR SALON.

4 When you do get through to this human resources manager or person in charge, try to actually schedule the appointment to discuss the matter in your salon rather than at the company's offices. If this manager agrees to visit you, ask, "Can we discuss my plan while we're giving you a complimentary haircut, just so that you see the quality of our services?"

5 Whenever the appointment does take place, whether at the salon or in the company's offices, explain that you'll give all employees of the company, upon presentation of their corporate ID, a special incentive. You fill in what this incentive is. It can be a certain percentage discount,

a free piece of retail merchandise of *your* choosing, a free manicure, a facial treatment, or whatever you feel is appropriate.

6 If the human resources person agrees, ask him/her to send out a bulletin, or have a notice prominently posted on their bulletin boards or noted in their company publication.

7 You can be as generous as you'd like and make any restrictions you'd like. For example, if you are already booked to capacity on Saturdays, make your offer valid only on weekdays.

8 Don't be discouraged if you get turned down by a few companies. Despite their external bravado, many corporate types are insecure, frightened, and timid about trying new things. Once you get one or two companies lined up, however, and word starts to get around, instead of being a little scared about trying your plan, they'll be a little scared about *not* making it available to their employees. You can't win them all, but once you start the ball rolling, they'll be coming to you as often as you'll be going to them.

9 A variation of all this is to offer that certain of your salon services be performed right there at corporate headquarters rather than in your salon. Men may be particularly attracted to this arrangement. You can do a few haircuts and trims while they're in one of their lunchtime conferences discussing earth-shattering corporate strategies.

10 Once you really get in with one of these companies, you can start on a few more promotional strategies. Things like asking the company to offer a prize of "A Day of Beauty" to the employee of the month. The possibilities are endless.

People in offices show up for work in the morning and spend every day interacting with the same, or even a revolving, group of people, day after day after day. If you make a significant change in the appearance of only one employee, it will be immediately noticed and make for scintillating water-cooler talk. Everyone will want to know, "Where'd you get that haircut? You look beautiful!" And that's all you need. Boom! You've got dozens more clients.

IF YOU MAKE A SIGNIFICANT CHANGE IN THE APPEARANCE OF ONLY ONE EMPLOYEE, IT WILL BE IMMEDIATELY NOTICED AND MAKE FOR SCINTILLATING WATER-COOLER TALK.

Build Your Business When You're Not Busy

NETWORKING

It is the rare salon that's busy five days a week, fifty-two weeks a year. There are always slow seasons, slow weeks, slow days, slow hours. The worst thing that stylists or owners can do is "sit around." Just the thought of it is depressing, isn't it? People just waiting, waiting, waiting, when they could be doing productive tasks that can actually bring people in. There are, of course, things to do such as cleaning the stations, organizing the rollabouts, or reading beneficial articles in trade magazines, but why not do things that can be beneficial in a more tangible way—like building business and attracting clientele. Here are a few things that can be done.

1 Keep in touch with existing clients. Call a few that you've done recently.

- Thank them for coming in.
- Tell them you have a few spare moments and are just following up to make sure that all went well.
- Check if the color, cut, perm has been easy to work with, easy to maintain.
- Ask if they'd like to schedule their next appointment.
- Tell them you'll appreciate a recommendation to their friends.
- Thank them again.

2 Visit a few stores in shopping areas within a mile of your salon.

- Introduce yourself to owners and employees who aren't occupied with customers.
- Invite them to the salon for a personal tour of your premises and exposure to your services.
- Always leave your business card. Even if they happen to be busy and not able to give you time, leave your card. There's no less expensive way to advertise.

3 Study the Yellow Pages for businesses that offer possibilities for cross marketing and/or mutual promotions.

- Contact the owner by phone.
- Tell him/her you'd like to explore building his/her business and your business by crafting a promotion beneficial to both.
- Don't go into too much detail on the phone. Explain that details can be crystallized person to person when you meet.
- Invite the owner to visit your salon for a tour, a conversation, and perhaps a sampling of your services.

4 Scour your local newspapers for news about groups and organizations that might be interested in group discounts or lectures by you or members of your staff.

- Call the president or chairperson of the group. Explain what you have in mind, but, again, don't go into great detail.
- Invite the person into the salon for a personal conversation, tour of the facilities, and determination of a plan you have in mind.

BEING A SALON
HYDRAULIC CHAIR
POTATO BUILDS
NOTHING, ADDS
NOTHING.

There you have it. Not a promotional plan to jump up and down about or have Hollywood spotlights lighting the sky for, but nonetheless a plan that can result in business. Being a salon couch potato or, more appropriately, a hydraulic chair potato builds nothing, adds nothing. On the contrary, it's a minus. It drags you down. There's absolutely no doubt that doing any of the activities noted above will result in business. They *will* help business. But let's be pessimistic and say they don't. It's still a net gain. You've met new people. You've distributed cards. You've spoken to clients, you've been *doing something*! It's a learning experience! What do you learn by sitting around? Point made.

Break the Ice with Men's Clubs

Many salon owners have caught on to the idea of lecturing to women's clubs to expose the salon and its stylists to women in the organization. This is a wonderful idea and never fails to generate new business. But why confine yourself to only women's clubs? Why not men's clubs, as well?

NETWORKING

1 Ask around among your clients for the names of various local organizations their husbands, sons, boyfriends belong to. You don't need a lot of them. To get started you only need one or two. Contact an organization's president or program chairman and offer your professional services at one of their meetings.

2 Just in case you don't know, men are interested in their appearance! Men are vain! Men want to look as youthful as they can! And dashing, too! Men have loads of questions about thinning hair, graying hair, styling, and on and on. *You* have all the answers. You can even tell the president or program chairman that the title of your presentation will be "Everything You've Always Wanted to Know about Hair But Didn't Know Whom to Ask."

JUST IN CASE YOU DON'T KNOW, MEN ARE INTERESTED IN THEIR APPEARANCE!

3 If you get "booked," prepare a presentation for whatever time you're allotted. Try to keep the whole thing down to about thirty to forty-five minutes, including questions and answers. If it's much longer than that, people get fidgety. Start with some generalities like how fast hair grows, the structure of hair, male pattern baldness, and so on. Ease into haircolor, semi, demi, and permanent. When you talk about haircolor, assure them that they can phase into coloring their hair over a period of several months so that no one will be able to spot the process. Try to find someone in the audience with a decent head of hair and have one of your stylists cut it as you discuss the procedure of analyzing the face, cutting to the bone structure, et cetera.

4 Make sure you touch on just about every conceivable service you have available for men, even if you only cover some subjects fleetingly. The more subjects you touch on, the more questions the audience will think of asking.

5 Whatever time you're allotted, make sure to leave fifteen minutes for questions and answers. If you know any of the men in the audience, try to plant at least one or two questions in advance just to get things started. Before answering *any* question, *always* repeat the question. When giving your answer, if possible, point to specific people to illustrate your answer. You won't be doing this to embarrass anybody, but it will stimulate a certain amount of interest and kidding when the answers have personal applications in the group.

6 When you have established your expertise and have gained real rapport with the group, spontaneously suggest that you'd love to see some of the men come into your salon. Suggest—again spontaneously—that if they mention they are members of the particular club or organization, you'll be delighted to give them a 20 percent (or whatever) discount on their first visit.

7 If the time flies by and there is obvious interest in the room and you're running out of time, ask them if they'd like to have another session some-time in the future exclusively devoted to perhaps one specific subject they seem to have a lot of interest in or curiosity about. If they like the idea, tell them you'd be delighted to come back.

8 Either by putting one of your business cards on everyone's chair in advance or by having one of your staff pass out your cards, make absolutely certain that every man in the room walks out with one.

If you've prepared well, rehearsed well and done a program that is perhaps even a little shorter than the audience thought it would be (rather than a little longer than they feared it would be), you'll walk out of the room with an absolute reservoir of goodwill.

Yes, some of the men will automatically drift back to the establishments they've been going to for the last twenty years, but you can be assured a certain proportion of them will be delighted to have made your acquaintance and will call you during the next few weeks. Who knows, some of the men may even be impressed enough to recommend you to their wives.

Tie In With
a Photographer

NETWORKING

Promo
46

Not every salon has a photographer nearby. Ideally, for this promotion you ought to have one within distance or only a few minutes' drive. If you don't have a photographer in this kind of proximity, this promotion is probably not for you. Go through it, however. It may spark other ideas or ways you can tie in with photographers. If you do not have a photographer within shouting distance, you can materially help his/her business and he/she can help yours.

Before any commercial photo shoot with professional photographers and professional models, a great deal of attention is paid to the model's makeup. There's always a makeup artist on the premises to see that the job gets done properly. The all-important makeup factor is never left in the hands of the models themselves. Yet with local photographers the makeup job is considered the responsibility of the person being photographed. The photographers realize this shortcoming in the whole procedure, but they really can't do anything about it. They can't each employ a full-time makeup artist. Aha! That's where your salon comes in. Here's what to do.

1 Visit your photographer neighbor or invite the photographer to your salon for a chat. Propose that the two of you contribute equally to have a gift certificate given out at his studio, entitling the bearer to a free total makeup session at your salon before the portrait sitting.

2 Suggest that while the makeup would be free to the subject, it would actually cost the photographer $5. Explain that this would certainly not cover the cost of a complete makeup session, but you at least need a contribution from him to help toward your time, effort, and materials costs.

3 The photographer can certainly feel free to advertise or promote this free makeup session with each portrait sitting, which can be an excellent promotional incentive. Even if this offer attracts only a few additional sittings, it will more than pay for the $5 outlays.

OFFER A FREE MAKEUP
SESSION BEFORE A
PORTRAIT SITTING.

4 It goes without saying that $5 won't cover the time, effort, and materials for a complete, from scratch makeup session. But consider this: When the subjects (usually, but not necessarily, women) schedule their free session, they will very often book a shampoo and style or cut, manicure, and possibly even perms and colors—all at standard salon prices.

5 Have a small display sign made up in the salon telling your clients about this free makeup session when they schedule a sitting with the photographer. At the same time, have the photographer make a sign for his studio telling prospective clients about the free makeup session in your salon. One hand washes the other.

6 Of course, to consider this promotion at all, you must have at least one cosmetologist, preferably more, who is really knowledgeable about make-up techniques, facial bone structure, day makeup, night makeup, and glamour makeup. If the makeup person does an "ordinary" job, the subject may be disappointed, the photographer maybe annoyed, and it will all be a net minus. The best idea is to have several people study, practice, work on each other and really elevate their makeup art. When that's all in place, you're ready for all comers.

This is one of those relatively simple promotions. The monetary outlay is virtually pennies. And yet if the photographer is good and your makeup people are good, it can bring several dozen new clients in over the course of the year. This adds up to thousands of dollars in revenue. No fireworks, no drums, no fanfare. Just a quiet and fun way to fatten your bank account.

Cut, Color, Nails

Cutting Marathons

Promo
47

CUT

You've heard, seen, or participated in "cut-a-thons." Actually, the word is copyrighted, and while I don't imagine anybody has ever gotten into real trouble using that word, there are those who've received letters to cease and desist. So I prefer to call them by the longer designation, "Cutting Marathons." There are endless variations, and you pretty much have to determine which one feels right to you.

1 Consider the charity that will benefit. Keep in mind what Tip O'Neil, the last great majority leader of the House of Representatives, once said, "All politics are local." By this he meant that while people were interested in the big issues like foreign policy, education, and the economy, when it comes time to vote, we cast our ballots for politicians who will help solve strictly local problems—giving government aid to rebuild from a local disaster, keeping local streets and roads passable after snowstorms, converting a rundown empty lot into a park or playground. The same holds true with charities. Yes, the big national campaigns for AIDS research or breast cancer are notable and laudable, but people may respond more enthusiastically to a fundraiser to send the high school football team to the regional championships or for an especially needy family that suffered hardship or loss. The choice is up to you; the cause is up to you.

2 You must have the cooperation of every cutter on your staff. It has to be a full team effort. If half of the staff doesn't want to go along, pass on this kind of promotion, and over the course of months try to influence their opinions to a more favorable reaction.

3 Where to hold it? Obviously, it can be in the salon, but you'll generate more crowds if you hold it outside. This can mean on the sidewalk outside the salon or in the parking lot or in a public park if that's permitted.

4 The kind of money you raise will depend on several choices.

• You can charge full haircut prices and do no services other than haircuts on that given day, and donate all proceeds to the charity.

Indeed, clients can make their checks out directly to the charity, thus getting themselves a tax deduction. You and your cutters may also be entitled to deductions based on the amount of labor you put in and income you have sacrificed. Make sure you check with your accountant on all IRS possibilities. In this particular variation of the haircut marathon, you'll mostly attract your own existing clients, but it will engender lots of goodwill and favorable publicity.

- You can bring high stools or director's chairs outside the salon, but obviously you'll need to shampoo clients' heads inside before you bring them outside for cutting. Needless to say, you've got to do this in a good-weather time of the year. If you're not in the salon setting, you shouldn't charge in-salon prices. You can cut your prices in half and again have the checks made out directly to the charity.

- Sometimes you can run your cutting marathon in advance of, and in conjunction with, a community or charitable event being held in the local park or playing field. Maybe there will be fireworks. Maybe a rock band is scheduled. People want to get good seats, so they start arriving an hour, or two or three, in advance. You can approach the producers, and ask if you can schedule your cutting marathon for those few hours when people start arriving. It will give the folks something to watch before the official festivities. You and your staff will be on stage, and you can make the charge a donation to the community or charity. ("Be as generous as you can" should be the guiding rule.) You'll attract plenty of takers, and your name will be known to every person attending the event. When each haircut is completed, have the client stand, turn around, and take a bow along with his/her stylist. That's a lot of bows, a lot of applause. Again, check with your accountant to see what kind of deduction you can take for time, supplies, transportation, and who knows what else.

5 As always, take pictures. Try to get publicity and coverage in local media before and after the event. If nobody publishes your story, you can always blow your own horn by putting photos in your window along with accompanying captions explaining who, what, and where in each photo. Believe me, people will come by to stop and stare.

Community activity of this nature is enormously rewarding even outside of the new clientele it may attract. We are in a service business, a people business, a feel-good business. Our job is to make other people feel good. When we do that and contribute to the community and/or a worthwhile charity at the same time, we make ourselves feel good. This alone is a wonderful gift to ourselves.

The Second Haircut Is Free

CUT

One of the toughest clients to satisfy 100 percent is the first-time hair-cutting client. She comes to you because she's unhappy with the haircuts she's been getting elsewhere, but right away that can present problems. You may not be able to overcome the design the previous haircutter put in. Or perhaps the hair has been damaged by either home treatments or work done in another salon, but you can't cut all the damage off—that may make the hair too short—so you have to work with what you've got and do the best you can. Or the client has seen a haircut you've executed on someone she knows, and she wants you to duplicate it on her. Trouble is, her hair is different and her face is different. The cut you give her may actually be right, but it may not be exactly what she had in mind. The list of problems goes on, but the conclusion is that it's tough to get that cut exactly perfect the first time—and who knows if she'll give you a second chance. "The Second Haircut Is Free" idea is a way to lock clients in.

1 You must explain the rationale behind this promotion to all your cutters. Normally if you ask them to do a haircut for nothing, they would be annoyed. But when you explain that this free haircut is going to boost their retention rate enormously, they'll go along.

2 Everyone must know the rationale and must get it down cold. It is that haircutting is a fine and complex art; sometimes in familiarizing oneself with the hair and the client for the very first time results may be satisfactory, maybe pretty good, maybe even excellent, but they're usually not perfect, not exactly on target.

The stylist should say to the client, "You may be perfectly satisfied, but I see improvements I'll be able to make once the cut grows out for a few weeks. And because our goal in this salon is to achieve results as close to perfection as possible, we offer the client the second haircut for free." The second time the stylist will be more familiar with the client and the way her hair grows and will be able to make minor adjustments so that the cut is even more satisfactory not only to the client but to the haircutting artist, as well.

3 You can print coupons to give to first-time haircutting clients so that upon presentation, the next haircut will be free. To make it even simpler and involve no printing costs whatever, the stylist with the first-time client can write on the back of his/her business card, THERE IS NO CHARGE FOR MRS. JONES' NEXT HAIRCUT. Then the stylist signs it.

Think of the dynamics here. How often does it happen that a first-time client smiles, says "Thank you," and is never seen again? She gets home and in a day or so her hair isn't looking exactly the way she wants it to. Negative feelings set in. "Maybe I'll try another salon next time." That second-haircut-free coupon or card stops this negativism in its tracks. Instead, the client thinks, "Well, the stylist explained this to me, and I'm certainly not going to pass up a free haircut. I'll give her another shot. I've got nothing to lose."

YOU HAVE A SECOND CHANCE TO SATISFY THE CLIENT; MAKE THE MOST OF IT.

When she comes back for that second cut, she'll be candid. She'll tell you exactly what she didn't like after she got home or what happened to the style after she shampooed it and had to take care of it herself. Normally you might not get a second chance. Now you have it, and you can make the most of it. You can address all the problems the client articulated. The line that will be growing out is the line that *you* put in. It wasn't put in by some other, possibly less competent, haircutter.

Do you have the confidence in yourself to know that in two haircuts you can produce total satisfaction? If so, this policy will boost your retention rate for haircutting clients to just about 100 percent.

Caution: Stylists must guard against thinking or grumbling that this policy simply cuts the price of a haircut (and therefore their commissions) in half. Sure it does, but it does something else. It assures that the client will come back for the third haircut and the fourth and fifth and tenth—and all at regular prices.

Another phenomenon takes place, as well. When the client knows that she is getting an absolutely free service, her tip to the stylist will be larger, and she'll likely avail herself of another salon service or some retail products. Psychologically it works out that way.

In the long run—and the long run means by the client's third visit—everyone is ahead of the game, including the client. And that's what counts.

Make Monday
Blonding Day

COLOR

ON MONDAYS YOU DO

NOTHING ELSE BUT HAVE

BLONDING SERVICES.

Elsewhere in this book is the suggestion that you may want to stay open on Mondays. There are persuasive reasons for you to do so. Perhaps, however, you don't want to commit yourself. You may want to test the waters. If so, you can stay "partially" open by making Monday a "specialization day."

Let's take for granted that except for individual corrective problems, the haircoloring service that requires the most attention, and is most time-consuming is blonding. Clients know this, too. They know it takes time and special attention to get the perfect blonding result and keep blond hair in good condition. If you have an abundance of blonding appointments late in the week, it's nice to welcome the business, but it puts a lot of pressure on everyone. Let's relieve some of that pressure on the one hand and build your blonding business on the other. Let's make Monday "Blonding Day." That doesn't mean you can't, or won't accept blonding service appointments on any other day. It only means that on Mondays you do nothing else but have blonding services and whatever finishing services you have to do on the hair after the blonding. Here's how to work it:

1 Sit down with your staff to make sure that several of them who are adept at blonding work are willing to come in on Mondays when the promotion starts drawing a Monday clientele. Some may be happy to do it to earn extra money. Some may want to trade off coming in on Monday and having time off later in the week. Or you may be able to hire competent people who prefer to work only on Mondays. All this will come out when you explain to your staff what you are trying to do and how it will benefit the salon, the haircolorists, and the clients.

2 Put a sign in your window or send out postcards or give out flyers or do some local advertising that says something like:

MONDAY IS BLONDING DAY!

Are you a blond?
Do you want to be a blond?

Dimensionalized Blond,
Naturalized Blond,
Carmelized Blond,
All-the-Way Blond,
Touch-of-Blond,
Have-More-Fun Blond?

Blonding is serious business. It takes lots of know-how. Our specialists have plenty of that. But it also takes *time*, and Monday is our take-your-time day. You'll get careful, personalized, individualized attention so that the blond you become will be not only beautiful but perfectly conditioned. On Monday we think of nothing except glamorous blonding results. Come blond with us.

3 You've got to "pay off" on those promises. You must work slowly, carefully, meticulously, and offer lots of personal attention to those blonding clients. They have to feel a difference between a Monday appointment and a Friday appointment.

4 Pay particular attention to conditioning. On Saturday you may be satisfied with achieving the color result and getting the client out of the chair. On Monday the conditioning must become equally important.

5 As an extra inducement or icing on the cake, you may want to offer either a discount on Monday blonding services or include a free retail product with each appointment. You don't have to do this forever. Once the Monday book starts to fill up, you can withdraw these goodies.

PEOPLE WHO ARE NOT
YET YOUR CLIENTS MAY
HEAR OF YOUR POLICY
AND DECIDE. "THESE
ARE THE EXPERTS."

Making Monday a specialization day will not only even out your week and bring more business in, but you will become known as a salon that knows what they're doing on blonding. People who are not yet your clients may hear of your "Monday is Blonding Day" policy and decide, "These are the experts. I'll go to them with my questions, my problems." Your business the rest of the week will fill in soon enough, and all the while you'll have six days of income instead of only five.

Haircolor
in Minutes

Promo
50

COLOR

DON'T LET LIMITED-

TIME-AND-MONEY

CLIENTS ELUDE YOU.

THEY CAN ADD UP TO

BIG BUSINESS.

Professional haircolor has truly become an art form. It wasn't always this way. Years ago most coloring was done to cover gray. It consisted of: Pick the right color; apply to the roots, thirty-five to forty minutes; pull through the ends, five to ten minutes; rinse; fini. Not much art there. But nowadays colorists will use three to five color shadings on one head, beautifully dimensionalized with small partings, weavings, patterns, tin foil. What emerges is not only art but a service that simply cannot be duplicated at home, even by a gifted amateur. That's the good news. More good news is that many women are willing to spend the money and the time to get these beautiful services. The bad news is that although there are many potential clients for these beautiful, artistic color services, a good many may *not* be willing to devote the time required and/or they may not want to spend that much money. Don't let these limited-time-and-money clients elude you. You can still get them, and they can add up to big business. What you've got to do is devise several different quick-color techniques to do the job, get the money in the till, and get clients on their way. Here are three techniques to get you started. You and your colorists can probably devise several more.

Air Brushing.
Use a plastic bristle vent brush and a tint that's one to two shades lighter than the client's natural base. After the client has been styled, dip the brush into the color formula, then brush through the dry-styled hair. After about twenty minutes, rinse and restyle.

Scrunch Accents.
Use this technique on curly or wavy hair. Color formula can be two to three shades lighter or darker than the client's natural color. Wearing gloves, of course, lather the color in your hands and scrunch it right into the style, accenting the lower shaft.

Finger Weaving.
This is the simplest technique of all. Dip your fingers into a tint formula that is again two to three shades lighter than the client's natural color. Weave out pieces of hair, sometimes thick, sometimes thin. Highlight them with the color formula on your fingers, and leave on the hair for approximately fifteen minutes.

All these techniques will produce subtle highlighting, nothing radical—but, then, she won't be expecting anything radical. From beginning to end, each of these techniques will take no more than thirty minutes. The prices are up to you, but keep them reasonable. Remember, if the client likes what she sees, she'll want to do it again. After that, she may want something little bit more—a little bit lighter. Once she becomes a color client, she will—some way, somehow—find not only the money but also the time to spend on the real artistic haircoloring work you're capable of performing.

Once you and your colorists have determined which quick-color services you want to promote and feature, you've accomplished the easiest part of this promotion. The harder part is communicating it to all your clients. Take it step by step.

1 Meet with your staff and agree that you're going to go after every client who isn't receiving haircoloring service. Encourage each member of your staff to review their appointments early in the day to determine exactly who they'll target for the quick-color-techniques program.

2 Determine the exact wording you all feel comfortable using in approaching, describing, and proposing these techniques. "Ms. Jones, I know you're always in a rush, so I want to tell you about a wonderful new technique I've devised called color airbrushing. From beginning to end it'll take about twenty-five minutes. You won't see a big color change, but you will see beautiful, subtle highlights. I think you'll like it. Want to try?" Or, "Ms. Brown, you've got the perfect hair for a new color technique we've devised called scrunch accents. I do it with my bare hands. No partings, no tin foil, no long development time, but the results are subtle and beautiful. What do you say we try it?"

3 After about a month of speaking to targeted clients on a one-on-one basis, put up a sign in the salon simply saying:

BEAUTIFUL COLOR HIGHLIGHTS IN MINUTES!
All haircolor techniques do NOT take a lot of time.
Ask about our 3 new quick-color techniques . . .
AIRBRUSHING
SCRUNCH ACCENTS
FINGER WEAVING
Subtle, natural, shiny highlights IN MINUTES!

Between the new color clients you'll get by speaking directly to patrons plus the additional numbers you'll get as the information from the sign sinks in, you'll substantially increase your color business. Actually, it will enhance your relationship with clients simply by bringing these techniques to their attention, even if they say no to them. Countless studies have shown that clients look to their hairdressers for information about new techniques. They may not buy everything, but, believe it or not, they want to hear about everything even when they say no. You are their authority, and clients like knowing that you are staying state-of-the-art in all manner of salon services. So the success of this promotional device will actually be greater than the specific sales it generates. Confidence in your professional knowledge is one of the best business builders—and business keepers—you can engender. Capitalize on it, and reap the rewards.

CLIENTS LIKE KNOWING THAT YOU ARE STAYING STATE-OF-THE-ART IN ALL MANNER OF SALON SERVICES.

Five Sun Streaks
for Free

COLOR

There are clients whose hair fairly screams out for highlighting. Yet they won't do it. Are they happy with their dull, drab hair that's mousy or dishwater or "dirty" blond or brown? No. Yet they won't do anything about it. They're frightened, they're insecure. They have an infinite number of excuses. . . .

"It just wouldn't be me."
"I think my kids would laugh."
"I just don't want to fuss with it."
"My husband would kill me."
"Mother Nature knows best."

And on and on and on. The client *knows* her haircolor is unattractive. She'd love for it to be brighter, prettier. So why doesn't she do it? Who knows? It could be fear of the unknown, resistance to change, maybe a worry about the money it will cost. What we do know is that we haven't touched her "hot button." When you don't know which hot button to push, you can always rely on the good old standard: FREE! Now then:

1 Obviously, you're not going to do a highlighting job for free on every client that can benefit from it, but you can give out "samples." For a limited time—say a month or two or even on an ongoing basis—offer five free "sun streaks" to every client, regardless of the service they came in for. Whether she's there for a manicure, waxing, perm, or a cut, the offer stands for five free sun streaks.

2 Five highlighted wisps of hair won't do very much, but that's exactly the point. It won't scare clients away. It won't hurt at all. But *she* will see it. *She* will see that a teeny amount of highlighting won't make a drastic change, but it *will* make a difference, and she'll be pleased and appreciative. The cost is pennies; the time is minutes.

FIVE HIGHLIGHTED

WISPS OF HAIR WON'T

DO VERY MUCH, BUT

THAT'S EXACTLY THE

POINT.

3 Here is what can happen. Some clients will see that they can have color highlights without changing the color of their hair. This will reassure them and may give them just the boost they need to book a color appointment. Other clients will reason that if five little highlighted areas made a tiny but definite improvement, ten or twenty highlights would make that much more of an improvement. The point is that before the free streaks, they wouldn't even dip their toe into the highlighting waters. When they dip that toe in and find that the water's fine, a good percentage will be on the road to going all out.

4 Even the ones who don't opt for an immediate change will be appreciative of the gesture. People always appreciate a free service, especially if you don't push them hard for the full service. Next time the client comes in, give her another five. Surely someone is bound to say, "Your hair looks lovely. It looks brighter. Have you been out in the sun?" The first time she gets even a tiny complement, she'll be on the phone booking an appointment.

If you do this for a few months and manage to get only one or two new color clients out of the deal, it will have paid for all your time and trouble. Anything beyond one or two, you're way ahead of the game.

NOTES

Sure-Fire Haircolor Business Builder

COLOR

YOUR HAIR COLOR AND

THE HAIR COLORS OF

YOUR EMPLOYEES

EXERCISE AN IMMENSE

INFLUENCE ON YOUR

CLIENTS.

Years ago I called on the exclusive Lily Daché salon in New York City and was talking to the colorist. Suddenly she looked at her watch and said, "Sorry, you've got to leave." When I asked why, she told me Marilyn Monroe was scheduled as her next appointment. As I was being ushered out the door, I asked the colorist two questions that intrigued me about Marilyn's hair-color, "What's her formula, and how was it selected?" The answers? "Champagne Beige, and she chose it because she liked what it looked like on me." The moral of this true story? Your hair color and the hair colors of your employees exercise an immense influence on your clients. Let's put this influence to good use to help build your haircolor business.

How many employees do you have? Do they all color their hair? If not, they must be encouraged to do so. If indeed they all color their hair, are the results interesting? Are they exhibiting what's happening in the world of haircolor fashion right now? Are they wearing colors that would encourage clients to say, "I want that." Lets take it a few steps further.

1 Would I want to put myself in their hands? And even if some of the staff have beautiful color results, but they're wearing the same color month after month, year after year, it won't encourage clients with color to take a chance and try some different effects. We're at a point where fashion conscious women want to change color effects every now and then. When we change, it encourages them to also.

2 If everyone agrees (and everyone means men and women) cutters and colorists, nail artists and shampoo people—choose a day or two when everyone will get a coloring if they aren't doing it already, or will change their existing color. Generally, a Sunday or Monday are the best times. Everyone who comes in is either a "client" or a colorist's assistant.

3 Be certain to make refreshments, sandwiches, cookies, fruits and beverages available so no one has to leave the salon or take a break until everyone is done.

4 Don't just do color. Do cuts, restyles, makeovers, maybe even some perms (to illustrate that you can have your hair permed *and* colored). On Tuesday morning, and of course for days to come, everyone shows up with beautifully colored hair, finished hairstyles, and appropriate makeup. Will the clients notice? You bet they will. And they'll be impressed, and they'll comment about it. Will some clients miss the point? Maybe. So you might just take some Post-its and print NOTICE ANYTHING? in bold letters with a thick felt-tipped pen. Paste one of these notes at every station. Between the notes and the mass haircolor metamorphosis there will be plenty of good-natured commentary. That's what you want.

5 Once a color conversation is started, without pressure or pushiness, it can be steered into each particular client's needs.

- If the client is frightened because of potential damage, you could point out all the beautifully conditioned haircolor in the salon.
- If the client is starting to go gray but has been resisting, her stylist can point to the color effect on one of the staff and how subtle but real the improvement will be.
- If the client has mousy-brown or dishwater-blond hair, there will surely be several examples on how to enhance it.
- If the client has been having haircolor services, there may be a few examples for making some interesting color changes.
- If the client is adventurous, there will surely be some adventurous staff members whose hair color can be emulated.

The possibilities go on and on.

Your staff will be an ongoing model parade. Every client for least a month will be noticing many, many color changes since she visited you last time. You'll have more haircolor conversation during that month than you may have had for the previous year. And it's a fact of life that haircolor conversations lead to haircolor business.

It worked on Marilyn Monroe. It will surely work on your clients.

IT'S A FACT OF LIFE THAT HAIR-COLOR CONVERSATIONS LEAD TO HAIRCOLOR BUSINESS.

Two Quick Sentences to Help Build Your Hair Color Business

COLOR

YOUR CLIENTS DO

LISTEN TO YOU, DO

RESPECT YOU. ANY COM-

MENT FROM YOU ABOUT

THEIR APPEARANCE HAS

TREMENDOUS IMPACT.

All too often when people think of "promotion," they think of an expenditure of time, money, or both. Yes, indeed, a good promotion very often requires a lot of time and planning and the expenditure of money. But it doesn't always have to cost you the time or the money. Your clients do listen to you, do respect you. Any comment from you about their appearance has tremendous impact.

Obviously, we don't want to overtly criticize them or seem to be always pressuring them into another product or another service. No, we are their friendly counselors. "Counselors" means that we are going to give them competent, professional advice. "Friendly" means that we're not going to shove it down their throats.

Keep all this in mind when a client, who uses no coloring services, sits in your chair or any of the chairs in your salon. Her hair may be dull, drab, mousy, or dishwatery. But if you wait for her to ask for a little color, a little brightening, you'll wait a very long time—maybe forever. So, friendly counselor, you take a deep breath and in the friendliest manner possible say these two blockbuster sentences. Sentence #1: "Your hair's looking a little dull lately." Followed immediately by sentence #2: "How about a fast, nobody-will-ever-know color soap cap?"

That's it. No pressure. No sales talk. Just two sentences comprised of eighteen words. No one will ever give you a fast "no." Since they will have no idea what a "nobody-will-ever-know color soap cap" is, chances are they'll ask, "What's that?" Once you get the "What's that?" dear friendly counselor, you explain that it's just a coloring shampoo that will give the hair a little lift, a little life, and not require touch-ups. Some may decline, but surely half will express interest or give you an immediate OK or ask what the cost will be.

Whatever the outcome, you can't lose. Even if the client declines, you'll have created a certain awareness of how mousy, how dull, her hair looks. The seeds will have been planted, and two or three appointments later she may say, "You know, I think you were right. My hair *does* look a little dull. What was that you wanted to do?" More often they'll probably give you the go sign when you first say your two magic sentences.

It's up to you to decide what a color soap cap is. For many years people have been using a classic formula of one part color (whatever the appropriate tint shade would be), one part twenty-volume peroxide, and one part shampoo. Apply, leave it on a few minutes, rinse off. The most modern version of the color soap cap would be to shampoo with one of the new color shampoos that have been developed. They don't make a big difference, but if the proper color is chosen, it will give just that extra little bit of color so that when the client leaves the salon, her hair will be livelier than when she came in.

The best part of this entire procedure is that it gets you talking color to the noncolor client—and talking about it in the friendliest manner. It's not off limits any more, it's something you're talking about. Once you start talking, words like "highlights," "younger looking," "brighter," "livelier," and so on find their way into the conversation, and another recruit enters the vast army of people who have color in their hair.

Does this really qualify as a "promotion?" Think of every client in your salon who does not use a haircoloring service. Think of every stylist/colorist in your salon saying those two sentences and having friendly color conversations with each of the non-haircolor clients. Think of what percentage of these conversations will result in these clients starting to use haircolor. Then multiply the number of your probable successes by the average amount spent by clients on haircolor. Any way you slice it, we're now talking about *thousands* of new dollars. And it will have all started with, "Your hair is looking a little dull lately. How about a fast nobody-will-ever-know color soap cap?"

Call it anything you'd like. I'd call it one heck of a successful promotion.

Building a Manicure/
Nail Care Business from Zero

NAILS

Many salons do absolutely no manicure business. Are you one of them? There are always "reasons," and they range from not being able to find competent nail artists to not being able to compete with lower-priced nail salons. There are always problems, and you must endlessly look for solutions because a) there are profits to be made in nail services and b) women do want nail services. What a tragedy if a client can get permed, colored, cut, styled, and conditioned in your salon but has to go elsewhere to get her nails done. Many salons have lost clients this way. Here's a way out with minimum risk and a potentially enormous benefit.

1 Through your own contacts and by general asking around and networking, find a cosmetologist who simply can't, or doesn't want, to work on her own anymore but who is willing to learn and work and invest in herself. This person must either already be an accomplished nail artist or be willing to go to some of the many classes given by the various nail-care manufacturers in virtually every part of the country. The point is, if you're going to attempt to build a nail business, you must, at the very least, start with a very competent nail technician.

2 When you find her (or him, for that matter), make her a proposition. On your end of the deal you buy all the equipment products necessary to support a complete manicuring/nail-care business. The nail artist must agree to donate her time for thirty days, during which period all manicures will be given to clients for *free*. The nail person will surely get tips, and those will be hers.

3 After thirty days, it would be time to sit down with the nail artist and determine if the whole endeavor looks as though it's going to be worthwhile for both of you. If the nail artist is willing to continue, put her on at the same rate of commission you pay your stylists.

During the course of the trial month, the nail artist will have performed maybe two hundred or so standard manicures. Every client will now know that you're offering this service, and a couple of hundred will have received their free sample of it and be grateful for it. Out of this should come the beginnings of a nail clientele.

4 Keep your prices reasonable. You don't have to go to the rock-bottom level of your lowest competitor, but you shouldn't be light years above, either. If your prices are fairly reasonable, clients won't want to go through the inconvenience of going to another salon just to save a little bit on a manicure. Remember, you're just starting out. You can always raise prices later. At the beginning keep things low.

5 If during the second and third months the nail artist still has some down time, phase in a promotion whereby every cut or every color or every perm—gets a free manicure. After the first month you'll have established a base price for the nail service. So when you give it away for free, it will represent a real monetary savings in the mind of the client and will boost your cut or color or perm services.

If the nail artist is good, and the prices are right, before long she'll have a full book. At that time you can start to think about doing the whole cycle all over again with a second nail artist.

IF THE NAIL ARTIST IS GOOD, AND THE PRICES ARE RIGHT, BEFORE LONG SHE'LL HAVE A FULL BOOK.

Promo
55

Start a
"Nail Club"

NAILS

EVEN THOUGH IT'S

EASY AS PIE FOR

WOMEN TO PAINT THEIR

OWN NAILS, THEY

PREFER TO HAVE IT

DONE PROFESSIONALLY.

For many years many salons downplayed the manicure services and ultimately cut it out altogether. It was deemed "unprofitable." Well, evidently one person's unprofitability is another person's opportunity. Salons sprang up all over the country that specialized only in nails. There are countless incidences of a beauty salon in a strip mall not offering any nail services because of the perceived lack of profitability while several doors away a nail salon is booked to capacity. The fact is that even though it's easy as pie for women to paint their own nails, they *prefer* to have it done professionally.

But painting nails is only the beginning. This quickly graduates to broken nail repair and sculptured nails of all types and varieties. The cost of materials for nail services is minuscule, the profits extraordinarily high—providing you have the traffic. Well, you do have the traffic. Clients are coming into your salon for cuts, color, perms, conditioning. But no nails? That's a little silly, isn't it? Let's see if we can get some of those existing clients to become nailcare clients.

1 Hire one or two people who really know the business of nails, really know a variety of nail services. Conceivably you may not have to hire people. There may be a nail artist or two who would like to rent space in your salon for nail services and pay you a monthly rental fee. By and large, having your own nail artist(s) is the better idea. Once one gets busy, you can hire a second, then a third, and so on. Under most circumstances it's best to have complete control over all service people in your salon.

2 Print a small card the size of a normal business card that says:

Name of Salon
NAIL CLUB
Address of Salon
City, State
Telephone Number
After 6 Manicures Your 7th is FREE
| 1 | 2 | 3 | 4 | 5 | 6 | FREE |

3 That's it. Simple. After six manicures the seventh is free. Give one of these cards to each and every client who walks through the door. Do it for three months, maybe longer. Do it at least until your manicurists are carrying a full book.

4 Each time the client has her nails done, don't punch out one of the numbers with a hole punch. That would enable some less than honest clients to punch a few of the numbers themselves, thus entitling them to the free manicure before they've actually had six manicures. Instead, have the nail technician initial each as the client gets successive manicure services. It would be rare that an unscrupulous client would attempt to forge the nail artist's initials.

5 Obviously you needn't stay with the one-free-with-six formula. If you're starting a manicure department from scratch, you may want to offer one free with three or two or even one. Or if your nail department is well established, and you'd like to lock in your nail clients, you can make it one free with ten or twelve.

However you work it, get involved in nail services. Don't walk away from nails. It has been proven all over the country that women are willing to have their nails professionally done. Yes, you must be very sensitive to price. Many nail salons charge budget prices. If you have an established hair salon, you needn't go down to the budget nail salon level, but you can't go too much above it, either. Clients having their hair done in their regular salon will very obviously consider it a great convenience to have their nails done there, too. They will be willing to pay for this convenience, especially if after several manicures they get a freebie.

GET INVOLVED IN NAIL SERVICES. DON'T WALK AWAY FROM NAILS..

An Easy Way to Build a Nail Extension Business

NAILS

WHY SHOULD SO
MANY OF THOSE
WOMEN GETTING THEIR
HAIR DONE IN YOUR
SALON BE UNHAPPY
ABOUT THEIR NAILS?

It's a fact of life that many women are unhappy with their nails. They just don't like the way they look. Ask many women outright to show you their nails, and they'll either make a fist or put their hands behind their back. They see beautiful nails in the cosmetic ads and know their nails aren't in that league. But you and I know that a good, creative, artistic, technically competent nail artist can make *anyone's* nails look beautiful as the ads, sculpture them to any shape and length they'd like. So why should so many of those women getting their hair done in your salon be unhappy about their nails? Let's do something about it.

1 We must start, as with many of the promotions in this book, with the fact that technically proficient practitioners are an absolute must. The person or people charged with building the nail business must know their art and know it well. If you have those people already on board, we can go on to the next step.

2 When any of the nail artists has any open time at all, she should go from person to person in the salon saying, "I'm giving away a free nail today. Would you like one?" She can speak to clients in the waiting area, at styling chairs, under dryers, and those who are color developing. The normal reaction people have to getting *anything* free is, "Sure, why not?"

When a hairstylist or colorist wants to induce a client to try a new service, the stylist or colorist is always at somewhat of a disadvantage. The finished effect can be described, the client can imagine what the finished effect will be, but the client can't *know* what that finished effect will be until the service is completed. The nail artist doesn't labor under this disadvantage. By doing one nail, she can *show* the client what her nails will look like when the service is completed.

3 When anybody has a reaction indicating willingness, the nail artist takes her over and does a beautiful extension application on one finger. When the client compares that new nail extension to her other nine fingers,

she'll see what a dramatic improvement a full set of nails will make, and—viola!—You've got a nail extension client.

If your nail artist does this every time she has a spare ten minutes or so, it won't be very long before she'll have no spare time as all. That will be the time for you to hire another nail artist and start the procedure all over again. What a lovely little promotion! It's quiet, fun, good-natured, simple, and cheap. When you have a nail artist who is fully booked, you've got a very heavy contributor to your profits. With this promotion there will be absolutely no excuse, no reason, *not* to be fully booked.

SHE'LL SEE WHAT A DRAMATIC IMPROVEMENT A FULL SET OF NAILS WILL MAKE, AND—VIOLA!—YOU'VE GOT A NAIL EXTENSION CLIENT.

Retail,
Parents/Kids

Free "Built-In" Conditioning Treatments Will Boost Retail Sales

RETAIL

Nowadays practically every client needs some form of hair conditioning. It goes without saying that haircolor clients and perm clients surely need conditioning, but nonchemical service clients need it, too. Sun, salt water, chlorine, pollution, overshampooing, and overblowing all take their toll. This accounts for the incredible amounts of conditioners that are sold at retail, a vast percentage of it is *not* bought in salons. Your clients may be walking right out of your salon and into the drugstore or supermarket up the block to buy conditioners.

The late Jon Guenter, the great haircolorist and educator, had his own solution to this problem. Every client that needed conditioning got it— *free*! He trained each of his stylists and colorists to convey to each of their clients the message that:

> I want your hair always to be in perfect condition. It's my responsibility to get it that way and to help you keep it that way. So whenever I perform any kind of service on you at all, if you need conditioning, you will automatically get it. If you need just light conditioning with a quickie conditioner and with gels, sprays, or mousses that have conditioning in them, you'll get whatever you need. And if your hair becomes severely damaged for any reason and you need heavy-duty., deep conditioning treatments, you'll get those, too—with my compliments.

Needless to say, all clients will enormously appreciate this service and attitude. It eliminates having to "sell" the client on a conditioning treatment on each visit. It eliminates clients having to give excuses because they don't feel the spending the extra money for your conditioning treatments when they have their own conditioners back home in their bathrooms.

Ah, but it also gives the stylist and/or colorists the opportunity to talk about conditioning with every client on every visit. It gives you the opportunity to do a conditioning evaluation and to "prescribe" and explain which conditioning treatments you intend to use and why.

YOUR CLIENTS MAY BE WALKING RIGHT OUT OF YOUR SALON AND INTO THE DRUGSTORE OR SUPERMARKET UP THE BLOCK TO BUY CONDITIONERS.

Inevitably the client will be impressed, inevitably she'll be appreciative, she'll buy one or another of the products you told her you're using. You aren't actually "selling" anything. You're merely telling her what you're giving her for free.

You've got to keep in mind that every product you use on a client's head is a free sample. If they don't know about what you're using, they won't know about its properties, ingredients, or uniqueness. The only time they'll get to know about product characteristics is when they read the labels in the supermarket or drug store. That's where a lot of your clients get their total education. They should get it from *you*.

If you handle it all in an educational manner, in a giving manner rather than a pushy, selling manner, you won't have to close the sale, clients will ask for the products.

How about all the "free" material you're giving away? In terms of cost, it's minimal. Right now you apply many hair care products to clients' heads without charge and without even thinking of it. Who would ever think of charging for the shampoo you use, or the gel, styling lotion, shiner, or spray? You give these products away without a word and without a thought. But when you employee the free-conditioning policy, you'll have the perfect opportunity to explain why and how all the products you use, not just the conditioners, have special properties that add to the look, feel, and condition of the hair.

Giving away free conditioning treatments will add very minimally to your expenses but will help enormously to bring in retail sales not only of conditioners of all kinds, but of shampoos, gels, sprays, shiners, and mousses. And all the while your clients will be thanking you for your generosity.

Remember, too, that your costs may be reduced by asking for some participatory cooperation from your distributor(s). Very often manufacturers give them allowances for promotional activities, and they may be willing to pass some of these allowances on to you.

If your distributor's a good businessman, he'll probably be eager to cooperate. After all, you're making a sacrifice to be able to sell more merchandise to clients. Why wouldn't the distributor be willing to make an equal sacrifice to sell more merchandise to you? Don't be shy about asking for help from your distributors. Believe it or not, they want to help.

The policy described above was employed in John Guenter's salon on a verbal, stylist/client basis. You can, if you'd like, print this policy on your calling cards or in brochures, window signs, advertisements. The softest, gentlest way is the conversational way. But if you'd like to make more of it, by all means get it across in any way appropriate to your salon.

John Guenter used to say, "The more I give, the more I get." This is a perfect example of this policy.

Put the Client to Work, and Increase Retail Sales

RETAIL

Many times we involve clients in services we are performing. We ask them to hand us aluminum foil or rollers or perm rods. They always willingly become part of the process. Part of their willingness comes from the desire to learn more about how to handle their hair. As they assist you, they ask questions, they learn. They don't mind doing this. They actually like to. (Many's the long-haired young woman who learned the technique of bending over, head between legs, brushing hair out vigorously, then flipping the head up to have the full-volume look so many of them covet.) The trouble with all of these activities is that while they result in a certain amount of increased goodwill, they don't necessarily increase sales. We can however, use a client's curiosity, eagerness, and willingness to help in the sale of retail hair care products.

Depending on the client, we may want to sell her a conditioner, a spray or two, mousse, gel, or all of the above. All for home use. There are techniques involved in the use of each of these products. The best way to teach a technique, is to put the product in the hands of the client, instruct her in the best way to apply it and use it, thus familiarizing her with the actual product you want her to buy. Here's how to do it.

WE CAN USE A CLIENT'S CURIOSITY, EAGERNESS, AND WILLINGNESS TO HELP IN THE SALE OF RETAIL HAIR CARE PRODUCTS.

1 When the time draws near for the product to be used, ask the client what, if any, similar product she uses at home. When she tells you, you may or may not be familiar with that product and its characteristics, and you can say some sort of variation of this theme: "That's a grocery-store product, and I'm not really familiar with it. I'm not sure it has the conditioning power [the holding power, the flexibility, the whatever] of the product I usually use for hair like yours. In any event, let me teach you how best to apply your spray [gel, mouse, conditioner] for maximum results."

2 Put your product into her hands, and tell her exactly how to use it. How to distribute it best, where to go heavier, where to go lighter, how to brush or comb it through to achieve the proper effect, and so on. There is professional technique with virtually every product application. You take it for granted, but there are always things about it you can teach your client that she doesn't know.

3 End up with: "The results you achieve should give you better conditioning [or better hold, longer lasting results, more economy, more flexibility]. If you don't get these kinds of results with the product you're now using, and with the techniques that I suggested, you ought to think of buying this product [the product you are featuring] next time you come in."

4 That's the end of the whole procedure. It's not pushy, it's not high-pressure. You've taught the client something, and you haven't tried to sell her anything except in the softest possible kind of way. Most of the time she'll say, "Well, look, I may as well buy this product now as long as you think it's that good, and you've taught me how to use it." Bingo! A sale is made! Even if she doesn't buy it, she'll appreciate the instruction. And who knows? She may indeed buy it next time.

It's well known that there are many cosmetologists who shudder at the word "sell." But even they ought to be comfortable with this technique.

Each cosmetologist who works in your salon handles somewhere between seven and fifteen clients per day. On each of them they use at least one, often two or three, different hair care styling products. If each stylist employed this technique on each client with at least one of the styling products they use, your shelves would be absolutely bare in no time. This is not fantasy, it's reality.

This is a promotion that won't cost a penny. You already have the merchandise. You're already using it on your clients. All that remains is to have a meeting that explains this entire procedure and gets everyone on board. Watch what happens when there are a few success stories where clients come back and tell their stylists something like, "You know, I used that mousse you suggested with the technique you taught me and I've been getting so many compliments. I want to thank you." A few stories like that and everyone in the salon will get with the program—and your retail sales will soar.

THERE ARE MANY COSMETOLOGISTS WHO SHUDDER AT THE WORD "SELL." BUT EVEN THEY OUGHT TO BE COMFORTABLE WITH THIS TECHNIQUE.

Gift with Purchase

RETAIL

One of the greatest promotional ideas in the last several decades was "Gift with Purchase" as featured, popularized, and exploited by the great Estée Lauder. When you bought a certain amount of Lauder merchandise, you got a free gift of legitimate, acknowledged value, absolutely free. When many of Lauder's competitors said that they simply couldn't afford to do it, Estee herself said that she couldn't afford *not* to. Now, of course, virtually all cosmetics companies employ this promotion. Why not try it in your salon?

1 You can elect to promote services or products. By and large, products will work more advantageously because virtually every client can use some of the products featured in your salon. If a client comes in for a certain service, and you want to trade her up to qualify for the GWP, there may not be an additional service that she's interested in. When it comes to products, however, there is such a variety that she can always find not one but several she can use.

2 A nice number you can go for is $25. Obviously, you can choose a higher level or lower. When a client buys $25 worth of retail merchandise, she qualifies to receive the free gift.

3 Is there a particular modest line or two that you especially feature? Talk to the manufacturer's representative or your distributor. Explain that it's a promotion to sell more of the product that they sell you, so they ought to participate, too. You may be surprised. They may donate free merchandise or give you an additional discount on your purchase or maybe even a check. Don't be shy. Ask for their help.

4 This is not a promotion that you should run continuously. One month is the ideal time. When it's over, you can let a couple of months go by and run yet another gift-with-purchase promotion different from the previous one. Have a different incentive gift, or, if you were promoting one particular line, try promoting another.

5 Don't lament that you have to "give things away." Look at the coupons you receive in the mail, look at the merchandise advertisements in the newspapers, walk through any department store. It all comes under the heading of "merchandising," and everybody does it.

6 How do you get the word out on your GWP promotion? All kinds of different ways. Try them one at a time. See which works best. Some of the methods you want to explore are doing a mailing to your complete client list, putting a sign in your retail area, and having the gift on display at every styling station to generate conversation. If you can get your manufacturer to co-op an ad, you can advertise in local newspapers or shopper's guides.

A by-product of the Gift-with-Purchase program is customer goodwill. When people buy Lauder merchandise and get those lovely Lauder gifts, they have good feelings toward the Lauder company as well as the department store they're buying from. Goodwill and good feelings are an absolute necessity to anyone running a service business. You'll generate them in great measure with your Gift-with-Purchase promotion.

Promo

RETAIL

Look around you. Merchants are selling combination packages everywhere and always have been. The furniture store advertises a sofa, two chairs, a coffee table, and a lamp at a special price. Restaurants have both à la carte prices and complete dinner prices. What is a complete dinner but a combination of soup, entrée, dessert, and coffee? The car wash says if you want to have not only the regular wash but an underwash, instant waxing, and sun protectant, you can get them all at a combination price. Soap companies do it, cosmetic companies do it, everybody does it. Why not you? Here are some considerations to keep in mind.

1 If you're a full-service salon, you offer shampoos, conditionings, manicures, cuts, perms, coloring services, makeovers, maybe waxing, maybe facials, and heaven knows what else. Put together two or three combination packages. Perhaps one can include a shampoo, cut, blowout, conditioning, and highlighting. Another might be a shampoo, perm, cut, and condition. You might have shampoo, scalp massage, cut, and blowout. How about a simple one? Manicure, pedicure, and foot massage. The combinations are endless.

2 When you put together your combinations, total the individual prices, then make the combo available at about 20 percent less. You know what they say: Make it up in volume. Surely the increase in business you'll get from performing multiple services on clients will more than make up for the discount you'll be offering.

3 When you have a client who routinely comes in for a haircut once every month or two, a perm twice a year, or even a good old-fashioned standing appointment for a shampoo and style. It means that you have failed to impress that client with your competency in at least a half dozen *other* services. Why isn't she getting her nails repaired and/or manicured in your salon? Why is she shaving her legs instead of having them waxed? Why is she getting skin care advice from a part-time housewife working at the drugstore instead of from you? If she's only getting the same service

THE INCREASE IN
BUSINESS YOU'LL GET
FROM PERFORMING MUL-
TIPLE SERVICES ON
CLIENTS WILL MORE
THAN MAKE UP FOR THE
DISCOUNT YOU'LL BE
OFFERING.

on every salon appointment, you are purely and simply letting a load of potential business walk out of your salon every time she comes for her "usual."

An attractive combination offer will automatically get her to try at least one more service, possibly two or three, depending on the combination. When she tries that extra service, in some instances she may not continue it on future visits, but in other instances she will indeed book at least one new service or more.

When you come right down to it, there are only two ways to increase the total revenue in your salon. One, you must attract more clients, and two, you must sell your existing clients more services. The combination packages concept brilliantly accomplishes number two.

Increase Retail Sales with Five Words

RETAIL

We all know that every client who goes through your salon uses a shampoo. Many use a conditioner. Most use a gel and/or a mousse. Many use a spray. But the sad facts of life are that they'll often leave your salon empty-handed, then go up the street to a drugstore or supermarket and buy their hair care supplies. What does the drugstore or supermarket do to earn your clients' hair care business? Nothing. You and your staff are in charge of your clients' hair. Indeed, you're responsible for it. Yet for any one of a dozen reasons, stylists don't attempt to make retail sales if clients don't initiate them. Let's try to change that situation without upsetting the stylists and their relationships with their clients.

During the course of every single salon visit having to do with hair, products are used. In each case there are reasons why specific products are employed. If you want to get some gunk out of the client's hair, you may use a stripping shampoo. If you want volume, you'll choose a specific mousse. If you want that style to stay just as is, you'll use a particular spray, and so on. The stylist knows why she's using a product for a specific purpose, but the client does not. That's what we've got to change. Five words can help ease into this new mode:

"This is what I recommend."

These are powerful words coming from you or your stylist. You determine what it is you think each client should purchase on each salon visit. It's usually not wise to try to sell a whole array of products on one visit. That may scare her off or even offend her. But as you go about performing your services, pick up a specific product, *put it in her hand*, and tell her, "I'm going to use this such-and-such product because I want to achieve so-and-so. This is what I recommend when you want to do it at home."

That's it. That's all.

If you've selected the right product for the right service for the right client, you've done that person a favor. Rather than the dozens of different brands she would be exposed to at the drugstore or supermarket—some of which might work for her, many of which might not—you've chosen the one product that is absolutely appropriate. Is it more expensive than the

FIVE WORDS CAN HELP EASE INTO THIS NEW MODE: "THIS IS WHAT I RECOMMEND."

supermarket brand? Yes, it is. But the client knows it's going to work. If she buys a cheaper product and it doesn't work properly and she doesn't get results, or she throws it away, where's the economy?

In addition to all that, she should know just by her ongoing relationship with the stylist that if she isn't totally, completely, 100 percent satisfied, she can bring the product back at any time, no receipt necessary, no proof of purchase, and you'll refund her money.

That relationship, that iron-clad guarantee, the knowledge that "this product will work on *my* hair" is worth something. They may be paying more, but they'll be getting their money's worth.

And it all starts with, "This is what I recommend."

Glazes Are a Quiet
Business Builder

Shine is a characteristic that every woman wants in her hair. Whatever the styles are—whether long or short, curly or straight, natural or colored—client's always want shine. Shine will never go out of fashion. The advertising catchphrase of the world's top-selling shampoo is "Hair So Healthy It Shines." Clients want shine; give it to them. Here's how to go about building business with hair that shines.

RETAIL

1 Talk to your distributors, all of them. Ask for whatever product(s) they carry that impart shine. This glaze will usually be a spray, aerosol, or pump, but it can also be some sort of finishing gel or pomade. Try them all. That may take weeks, but so what?

2 After you've gone through every shine product your suppliers carry, a winner, maybe two will emerge. It's easy for manufacturers to make extravagant claims for their products. Ignore the claims. The reality will only surface with use and testing in your salon.

3 When you have decided which is best, order a substantial supply. You should have a display at every styling station.

4 All stylists should be instructed to use the finishing glaze on each and every client. When this promotional activity starts, the use of the glaze should be explained to each client. Something like, "Mrs. Jones, see the way your hair looks right now? Now watch when I apply this such-and-such glaze. Your hair is really going to shine." That's it. You don't have to push, you don't have to sell. The product will sell itself. She'll probably say, "That's pretty amazing. I want to use it every day."

YOU DON'T HAVE TO
PUSH, YOU DON'T HAVE
TO SELL. THE PRODUCT
WILL SELL ITSELF.

That's not the end of it. Over the course of future visits, the conversation can be guided into the general area of hair health. For hair to show itself off to the best advantage, the glaze shouldn't be asked to do the job alone. There's the shampoo you use plus the conditioner, mousse or gel.

The glaze is only the hook, the incentive for her to buy all the hair care products you recommend because you were the one to show her how her hair could shine.

Some things in running a salon, in satisfying clients, in increasing retail sales, are complicated, but some are simple. This is one of the simple ones. No muss, no fuss, no spiel—just a demonstration of how a really effective professional product does its job. Over the course of the year these simple glazing application/demonstrations will materially increase client satisfaction, retail sales, and increased confidence in your professionalism. Not a bad combination, wouldn't you say?

"Unadvertised Special" Gets Mothers to Bring in Kids

Everybody likes to get an "inside deal." Here's one that gives this benefit to people and will result in building up your kids business as well as your regular business. It can also beef up your Tuesdays and Wednesdays so that you're not back loaded into the tail end of the week. The device is used extensively by department stores and it goes something like this:

PARENT/CHILD

1 Make up a neat, simple but highly readable sign at the reception area that says ASK ABOUT OUR UNADVERTISED SPECIAL FOR CLIENTS' KIDS (AND GRANDKIDS) ONLY. When they ask, tell them that on Tuesdays and Wednesdays you will offer a 25 percent (or 20 percent or 50 percent or whatever) discount on all services performed for customers' kids only.

2 Stick with the "exclusivity" of the offer. If they ask if they can get the discount for neighbors' kids or anything like that, say, "No, we can't afford to give it to everyone. This is strictly a special price for our clients' children and grandchildren." If the client asks, "Does this apply to my twenty-year-old daughter?" just smile and say, "Sure, why not?" After all, the object is to bring in new business, so who cares how old the "kid" is.

3 A heavy discount like something in the vicinity of 25 percent is a major incentive for mothers to book their children. Most salons aren't busy in the early part of the week, so why not fill those chairs? In short order, you'll find that a Friday client who wants to take advantage of the hefty discount by bringing her son or daughter in on Tuesday will, nine times out of ten, also switch her own appointment to Tuesday. This frees up a spot in the appointment book on a busy Friday and fills two spots (the child and the parent) on a slow Tuesday or Wednesday.

4 It won't be more than a few months before your Tuesdays and Wednesdays become fully booked. At that time, if you wish, you can terminate the promotion. In most cases, however, it'll be a good idea to keep it running. In addition to increasing your business and leveling out your schedule, it creates a lot of goodwill.

PEOPLE LOVE TO FEEL

SPECIAL. THEY LOVE

TO GET SOMETHING

THAT NOT EVERYONE

CAN GET.

People love to feel special. They love to get something that not everyone can get. They might even induce some of their friends to become clients just so they too, can take advantage of the "unadvertised special."

Little Kids Present Opportunities

PARENT/CHILD

After World Word II we had the baby boom generation. Babyboomers gave birth to the Generation X gang. And now *that* generation is producing babies. The point is that there are millions of kids around—and they all need haircuts. Some salons have a strong preference *not* to have kids on the premises, either as clients or as visitors, and that's OK. Tantrums are always a possibility, as is screaming, running around, breaking things, crying, and whatnot.

But there is another point of view. A lot of young mothers may have trouble arranging for child care while they're off keeping their salon appointments. If they can bring their kids, and if the kids can in some way be contained and amused, you may be able to attract young mothers who might otherwise go elsewhere.

But the bigger opportunity is to try to attract the business that the kids represent. Their hair grows quickly. At the beginning, parents will have definite ideas about when and how their hair should be cut. Later as the kids grow older and start to go to school, they'll have their own ideas about hairstyles. If the atmosphere is pleasant and welcoming to these youngsters, they'll want to have the job done in your salon. It's really not terribly difficult to make the atmosphere inviting.

THERE ARE MILLIONS OF KIDS AROUND— AND THEY ALL NEED HAIRCUTS.

1 Set up one station (or two) that's exclusively for cutting kid's hair. That station should be in the rear of the salon rather than the front. If it's up front, every client who walks in may stop by or make a comment or simply draw too much attention to the kids' service.

2 The station reserved for kids should be decorated differently. That can be up to you, your creativity, and your budget. You can put up a little multicolored fence around it. Have the styling chair upholstered in bright colors. Buy big cutouts of cartoon characters, and put them around for decoration. You can have children's books for the kids to browse through. Balloons are always appropriate.

3 A must: a TV and a VCR. Every kid, regardless of age, has a couple of favorite videos that they've watched endlessly but are always willing to see again, one more time. You'll need a library of about a dozen top videos. Or you can tune the TV to a kid's channel.

4 Take two Polaroids of each kid. Give the child one and post one on the wall. That's "recognition," and kids will eat it up.

5 Invariably, one or two of your stylists will have a special talent for getting along with children. Those are the ones to assign to the task of kids' cuts. They'll build a loyal clientele that will keep coming back to them for years.

6 Make sure you have a display of retail products right within the kids' station. These products can be special shampoos, bubble baths, gentle brushes, multicolored combs, and hair ornaments. When the kids take liking to one of these, they're sold. Their mothers will never say no.

That's all you need to do. Of course you can advertise, of course you can promote, but if you're patient, it will build on its own. Hundreds of women pass through your salon during the course of every month. They'll all see this bright, fun kids' area. If their kids need haircuts, you'll get them. If they don't have kids that age, they have friends who do. They'll tell them. It will build, and the nice part is that as each child outgrows the special little kids' area, your salon will be waiting to welcome them as young adults.

The First Thing to Do after the Kids Go Back to School

PARENT/CHILD

Early September is a rough month in most households. Kids have anxiety about going back to school, books have to be bought, clothes have to be bought, schedules have to be drawn. By the time everybody's washed, dressed, fed, and shipped off to school, most mothers are ready to collapse. Can anything be better to boost their morale than a relaxing visit to a full-service salon? Trouble is, mothers are so busy, they don't even think about it. Ah, but if you remind them, if you if invite them, if you attract them, they'll be willing to come in, plop into a chair, and say, "Do it." (Translation: "Pamper me. I need it.") Knowing all this, let's strategize a campaign to bring these women in.

MOTHERS ARE SO BUSY THEY DON'T EVEN THINK ABOUT BEING PAMPERED.

1 First, you must have a mailing list. It's vital that you be able to contact every person who has visited your salon during the past year, two, or even more. Then try to for other appropriate mailing lists. The PTA or womens' clubs may be willing to share their lists with you. Other merchants may be willing to trade lists. And there are always list houses that rent lists.

2 You're going to send the people on your list(s) a postcard. If your budget allows, make it as creative or elaborate as you like. If you're on a tight budget, you can get your message across strictly with type and very little art or photography. The main thing is the message.

3 The copy can read something like this:

THE FIRST THING TO DO AFTER THE KIDS GO BACK TO SCHOOL

The first thing to do after the kids go back to school is to come into The Beauty Box, relax, and let our experts pamper your beauty needs. A scalp massage, followed by a luxurious shampoo. Then a cut, style, and blowout will do wonders for your morale. A slow, tranquil facial is a peaceful, beneficial, therapeutic experience. Finally, a professional manicure and nail treatment will give you a glamorous lift.

That's it, that's the message. Mothers will luxuriate in the thought of the salon experience. At some point during all the pandemonium they'll think about it again, and when they've done all their school-related duties, they may decide to do something for themselves. That's when they'll remember that little postcard.

4 Your massage should not only be inviting, it should also contain some sort of incentive. This can be that one of the services in the "relaxation" package is free. Or you can give everyone who presents the postcard a small package of bath crystals. You want them to feel that they won't merely be indulging their own needs but actually be saving money, as well.

5 When you see any particular client especially enjoying herself and luxuriating in the treatments, you can make her an offer she absolutely won't be able to refuse. The school year is usually nine to ten months. Tell her that if she comes in for six of these relaxation visits, the seventh will be on you. Chances are that free visit will be sometime in June, just when the school year ends and summer activities begin. She'll look forward to it, and she will rationalize giving herself the luxury of the treatments during the course of the school year.

By putting this promotion into operation, you'll actually be doing a great service for your female clientele. Women have so many things to focus on during the course of the year that they often completely lose sight of their own needs. When you make this relaxation regime available to them, they'll realize that they deserve some rewards during the course of the year. During those wonderful salon visits they can redirect their focus. It will be on themselves—and they deserve it.

WOMEN HAVE SO MANY THINGS TO FOCUS ON DURING THE COURSE OF THE YEAR THAT THEY OFTEN COMPLETELY LOSE SIGHT OF THEIR OWN NEEDS.

"Expectant Mother's Club" Will Bring in Business

Promo
66

New mothers are wonderful clients. They generally socialize with a group of other mothers, and they do a lot of talking about a lot of subjects, including where they get their hair done. The period immediately after they give birth is a difficult one, what with coping with a lot of new problems and not having as much time as before to care for one's self and one's appearance. It's during this postdelivery period that the "Expectant Mother's Club" can bring you business, and here's how it works.

PARENT/CHILD

1 You can use very simple coupons to register women into the "club." These registration coupons should always be available in your salon. Post a sign that says:

EXPECTING?

KNOW ANYONE WHO'S EXPECTING?

REGISTER IN OUR EXPECTANT MOTHERS CLUB

FOR A FREE GIFT WHEN YOU GIVE BIRTH

2 Encourage pregnant clients and pregnant friends and relatives of clients to register, whether or not they're salon customers.

3 If they want to know what it's all about, simply say that they'll receive a "Gift of Beauty" after they give birth. Keep very tight records of all the due dates. Two weeks after the baby was due, call the new mother on the phone, congratulate her, and personally invite her to the salon for a complimentary "Shampoo & Style," "Cut & Style," or whatever. It should be a salon service that has to do with hair and makeup. A busy new mother probably won't take time out of her schedule for something like a manicure or even a free retail product. But when you offer a service where a new mother can come in and for a short while be pampered and beautified, she'll love it and she'll make the time to come in.

WHEN YOU OFFER A SERVICE WHERE A NEW MOTHER CAN COME IN AND FOR A SHORT WHILE BE PAMPERED AND BEAUTIFIED, SHE'LL LOVE IT.

As often as not, chances are she'll want to schedule a service or two in addition to the free services you're offering. That's a plus.

NOTES

If the new mother is not and has not been a client of your salon, you have a glorious opportunity to make her one. You're calling at a happy time, and you're also calling at a time when she hasn't been paying much attention to her appearance but knows she's been neglecting herself. She'll be effusively appreciative.

For every two new mothers who come in for your generous free services, chances are at least one of them will become a regular client. Hey, that makes the whole effort worthwhile.

A Plan to Attract Teenagers

PARENT/CHILD

It makes no difference whether they're boys or girls, many teenagers don't want to cut their hair. Every parent has been through this trial and tribulation period. It's never a happy time. It's not happy for the kids either. They want to please their parents (or at least get them off their backs), but they just don't want to get clipped. And they all know friends who have visited salons and asked for "just a little off the bottom," only to leave in tears when the stylist thought she'd give the client her money's worth by cutting more off.

Some years ago the lingerie industry promoted the "no-bra bra." Then there was the cosmetic industry that went through a period where young women were espousing the political correctness of not wearing makeup. Some companies started promoting "no-makeup makeup." You can borrow this philosophy and offer teens a "no-haircut haircut."

1 First, get a list of the high-school-age kids in your area. If you're not in a hurry, you can compile your own list over the course of months. Mention to every client that you want to put young people in the area on your mailing list, and would they please give you the names and addresses of their own sons and daughters as well as any other kids whose addresses they know. That's harmless enough, and virtually everyone will cooperate.

2 If you're in more of a rush, contact the principals, assistant principals, or other functionaries in the local high schools, and ask if you may have the names and addresses of their student bodies to add to your mailing list. You'll have to give them some sort of incentive, and a good one would be that you'll donate one, two, three, or five "Days of Beauty" to the school for use in any manner they'd like. The schools can use these prizes as fundraisers, incentives for one program or another at the schools, or whatnot.

BORROW THE "NO-BRA BRA" AND "NO-MAKEUP MAKEUP" PHILOSOPHY AND OFFER TEENS A "NO-HAIRCUT HAIRCUT."

3 Once you have your list, send a mailing to everyone on it saying something like this:

ANNOUNCING

THE NO-HAIRCUT HAIRCUT

ESPECIALLY FOR TEENAGERS!

We at Beauty Magic Salon know that teenagers have a love affair with their hair, and who can blame them? We also know that after a certain point hair can get scraggly, stringy, and unkempt.

So we've devised the "no-haircut haircut."

It starts with a shampoo and conditioning treatment because all hair behaves better and looks better when it's clean and conditioned. Then, with great precision, we trim off the frizzy ends and, never taking off even a fraction of an inch more than you want cut, we will style your hair so that it's easy to care for and terrific to look at. If you'd like, you can even come in for a free consultation so that we can tell you exactly what we're going to do when we give *you* your "no-haircut haircut." Don't just have it cut, have it styled.

4 Be sure to enclose price information in your message. Obviously, you should also include the name of the salon, address, and phone number.

5 When any of the kids call or come in, assign them to your youngest stylists. They'll just feel better about it if the person cutting their hair could be their sister's age rather than their mother's.

Is this a lot of trouble to go through just to get some teens to come in for a minimal service? After all, they're not going to become steady clients. Maybe not, but before you can blink and eye, they'll be showing up in wedding announcements and joining the work force, and they'll be looking for just the right beauty salon. If the "no-haircut haircut" was a pleasant experience, they will return as adults.

But the rewards of this type of promotion are not just in the future. Kids hang out in swarms. A fifteen-year-old, happy with her "no haircut haircut," will tell it to a dozen other kids. That'll bring in a few more, and if these go away happy, they'll spread the word even further. Going after them is great strategy both in the short term and in the long term.

A Back-to-School Promotion
That's Not for Students

PARENT/CHILD

August/September is a hectic time in all homes that have kids. The kids can be little ones or big ones, but it's always hectic. The emphasis during this time is always on the kids, the students who are going back to school. They need supplies, books, clothing, and a million other things. They have very specific desires, and parents have to buy precisely the items they specify. By the time the kids are finally out the door and on the way to school—be it elementary school, high school, or college—parents are absolutely frazzled. And of these frazzled parents, it's generally the mother who needs the most rest and rehabilitation. Let's help that poor person.

1 We can do that poor mom a great favor by running a "Back-to-School Special for Mothers." This can be announced in a simple postcard. You know your clients. You know the ones who have kids—practically all of them. So you send them all a little card that's headlined BACK-TO-SCHOOL SPECIAL FOR MOTHERS. You say something like this:

> It's over! They're gone! You shopped till you dropped. You got them the supplies they wanted and the clothes they wanted. You coordinated the whole back-to-school effort, and at long last you've shipped them off. They're back to school.
>
> Now, how about you? How about a hefty dose of tender loving care—a combination shampoo/cut/blowout with a fifteen minute scalp massage and conditioning treatment thrown in as a bonus? The whole works is [price], a saving of [amount].
>
> For a change let it be you who's pampered.

2 Obviously, you can reword that copy anyway you'd like, change the ingredients anyway you want. If you'd prefer, use local newspaper advertising instead of cards. Or you can send personalized letters. No one rigid format will work for every salon. You must always consider your own clientele and your own lines of communications with clients.

BY THE TIME KIDS ARE FINALLY BACK TO SCHOOL, PARENTS ARE FRAZZLED—AND IN NEED OF PAMPERING.

NOTES

The main thing is to recognize the universality of back-to-school time and the fact that it leaves mothers wrung out. When mothers are in this frame of mind, they'll appreciate someone being aware of their plight and willing to do something about it. That someone is you and your stylists. Your mothers will appreciate you.

New Teens
Beauty Clinics

PARENT/CHILD

Have you noticed? The population patronizing beauty salons is getting younger and younger. We haven't lost the seniors, those in the middle years, or the twenty and thirty somethings, but teens in unprecedented quantities have become fashion conscious and therefore potential salon clients. A casual browse at the magazine racks will disclose the trend. More and more, fashion, makeup, and hair messages are being beamed at the teenage population. No sense waiting around for them to discover you. Make yourself visible at the exact time kids are discovering they are teenagers. Run a "New Teens Beauty Clinic."

1 Start with the recognition that parents, teachers, *and* the kids know that there are problems. Parents and teachers don't want the kids grasping onto bizarre fads, unhealthy beauty habits, improper hygiene. The kids want to grow up, get into the fashion swing, and look good for their peers. They also know they have skin problems, and they'd love to receive some authoritative advice in this area.

2 Plan a program very specifically geared to twelve- and thirteen-year-olds. It will have to do with professional and at-home skin care, professional and at-home hair care, the right choice of haircolor, tips on keeping nails healthy, lots of advice on keeping hair in good condition. The program should last sixty to ninety minutes. Longer than that and they'll get fidgety. Don't hard sell on them starting to come to your salon. That can backfire and turn their parents and/or teachers off. If they're going to come, let it be because they are so impressed with your expertise and the program you present.

3 Make a great effort to have a young dermatologist be part of the clinic. It will add enormous authority to the program, and the dermatologist will surely realize that several new patients will be picked up as a result of the effort.

4 Once you have the program format planned, start spreading the word. As always, go first to your clients. Explain, by a sign in your window, flyers, and personal conversations, what you're doing. Ask if they know any teenagers who might be interested. Invite them.

MAKE YOURSELF VISIBLE AT THE EXACT TIME KIDS ARE DISCOVERING THEY ARE TEENAGERS.

5 Go to the middle school, junior high, or whatever school has the twelve- and thirteen-year-olds. Explain your New Teens Beauty Clinic. Explain that it is noncommercial, and no products will be offered for sale as part of the presentation and demonstrations. Check the school's curriculum. There may be particular classes, such as Health and Hygiene, where announcements of your clinic could be made. If possible, get a notice put on some bulletin boards stating that you're doing the clinic as a community service and admission will be free, but because of limited seating it will have to be by advance reservation and tickets only.

6 Depending on your location and the habits of your community, the best day to hold your clinic will probably be on a Monday, when your salon is closed. The best time will probably be right after school lets out.

7 Open up your salon as much as possible and rent chairs for the kids to sit on. When the clinic is officially over, invite everyone who wishes to stay and ask personal questions. At least half will do exactly that. Tell them that any time they have a beauty problem of any sort, they should feel free to call or come into the salon for further counseling and consultation. No charge, of course

8 When the clinic is over, start planning for the next one. What were the major areas of interest? What did the kids need most? What did they enjoy most? Could you accommodate more? Should you invite fewer students? Keep the pluses and eliminate the minuses.

9 How often to repeat your New Teens Beauty Clinic is up to the response you get. If you were oversubscribed, plan another in three to six months. If your attendance was disappointing, schedule another six months to a year from now—but with improvements.

You're not in business just for today. All new teens will eventually start drifting into salons. A few at the beginning and then in increasing numbers as they mature through high school and beyond. Sooner or later they'll become salon clients—somewhere. If they know your salon was a friendly place where they got authoritative information, great technical competence, up-to-the-minute styles, and retail products that do the job, where's the logical place they're going to go?

Another plus in attracting young people is that it livens up the salon. You don't want to be known as a salon that caters only to a specific segment of the population. That's dangerous. Clients should see that in your salon women (and men) of all ages come in. That will give them confidence that good things happens there—and indeed they do.

Daughter/Mother
Back-to-School Special

PARENT/CHILD

Starting right at the beginning of August you'll notice supermarkets, mass merchandisers, department stores, and others advertising "Back-to-School Specials." All this inescapable advertising puts everyone on notice that summer is coming to an end, and they've got to start thinking of preparing for school. This means not only school supplies but clothing and overall appearance. College kids will want to look as great as they can in preparation for the burst of social activities that comes with the start of another semester. High school girls, too, want to look great to their peers. As long as everybody is in this mode of getting ready, we ought to ride this wave. One excellent promotional idea is to focus not only on the schoolgirl but on her mother, as well.

1 We want to keep in mind that the needs of the daughter are very different from the needs of the mother, so we needn't insist that they both participate at the same time. Actually, they'll probably like it better if they're separated.

2 You can notify your clients about your promotion by a simple but prominent sign in the salon starting at the very beginning of August. If you don't have a lot of client traffic in August, notify everybody by a preprinted postcard.

3 The promotion should be that the daughter can participate anytime during the two weeks *before* school starts. The mother can participate anytime two weeks *after* school starts. The charm of this is that it's the daughter who really has to be taken care of before school. When the daughter has been shipped off to school, *then* it's the mother who needs taking care of.

4 What should the promotional "hook" actually be? It can be any sort of incentive, but one that seems to work especially well is giving away a free retail product (up to a certain value). When the daughter comes in for her appointment, she has her choice of any product in the salon. Same thing happens with the mother. The charm of making it any product rather than a specific product is that when each of the ladies comes in, they'll

FOCUS NOT ONLY ON
THE SCHOOLGIRL BUT ON
HER MOTHER, AS WELL.

ask you and your stylists for recommendations. This will give you all the opportunity to discuss the various properties of a whole range of products. The likelihood then is that each will not only avail herself of the free product but also buy one or two additional products. This can be a bonanza! Many stylists worry about selling. They don't like it. In this case, however, they will merely be trying to help with the selection of the free product for the mother and for the daughter.

5 If the daughter is of the age where she is going off to college, make sure you get her name and mailing address. Other than vacations, she's going to be gone the better part of a year. In a month or two she will surely have used up her supply of whatever product she got free on your daughter/mother special. You can write to her giving her your good wishes for her college career and telling her that you'd be happy to mail additional supplies of the product(s) if she would simply drop you a card. She can either pay for the product(s) with her own credit card or perhaps her mother's.

Always keep in mind that high school kids and college kids are your clients of tomorrow. You must constantly keep attracting a younger generation as you continue to serve the older generations. Daughter/Mother specials are a perfect way of doing this.

A Way to Attract
College Students

Promo
71

PARENT/CHILD

College students have a sense of what they want to look like, be it clothes, makeup, or hair. They read the fashion magazines and, of course, they copy each other. They feel that they have total control over the clothes they wear. If they don't like them, they don't buy them. If they get clothes as gifts and they're not precisely what they want, they simply won't wear them. They feel the same way about makeup. They know what they want, and they feel they can exercise total control in getting it. With hair it's different. They may know what they want, and they may convey it to the hairstylist, but then it's up to the stylist to deliver precisely what has been asked for. It's out of the client's control and completely in the hands of the stylist.

All too often the stylist delivers more than is asked for. It has happened to countless people. In fact, it's the complaint one hears about salon experiences more than any other: "I told him what *I* wanted; he did what *he* wanted." Even if it hasn't happened to a young woman herself, she's heard it enough about others so that she's gun shy. Rather than "risk" having too much hair cut off, she'll simply not have it cut at all, or she'll just do it herself.

If you can get her into the salon and satisfy her, she'll enthusiastically recommend you to all her friends who have the same fears. Here's a way to do it.

1 College kids get a substantial amount of time off during Christmas, Easter, spring break, and summer vacation. Starting about a week to ten days before vacation time, post a sign in your window and/or place some small ads in local newspapers saying:

COLLEGE KIDS
TRY OUR GUARANTEED HAIRCUT
GUARANTEED NOT TO BE A *FRACTION* SHORTER
THAN YOU WANT IT TO BE
OR IT'S FREE!

WHEN A KID GOES HOME

AND HER MOTHERS

SAYS, "BUT THEY

HARDLY CUT ANYTHING

OFF," YOU'LL HAVE A

VERY HAPPY YOUNG

CLIENT.

2 That message says it all. You don't have any sort of price or discount incentive involved. The only incentive is your *guarantee* that you won't cut off any more than they want cut off. That assurance is what they're looking for. (Of course, you and your staff have to train yourselves not only technically but mentally to listen to them *very* carefully and if necessary to take hair off only in snippets.) When one of these students goes back home and her mother says, "But they hardly cut anything off," you'll have a very happy young client.

3 You may ask why you should confine this promotion strictly to college kids. The answer is, you shouldn't. The object here is to attract college kids before they go home or to attract the attention of those who'll pass the word along to them. If they feel the message is for them, it will have more power than if it's a general message for everybody. Now, then, what happens when a high school kid says, "Does that guarantee apply to me, too?" The answer should be, "Sure. When would you like an appointment?" And what happens when a regular client who is thirty-something to sixty-something asks, "Can I have that same guarantee?" The answer should be, "Absolutely." Getting these questions from others means that even among your own clients, there's a certain amount of fear or insecurity about having too much taken off.

4 There's yet another way to handle this if you'd like to confine it strictly to college kids going on vacation. You could tell others that you're going to run the same Guaranteed Haircut deal for "all others" after the particular college break is over.

If you're in an area where there is a decent college population at certain times of the year, you definitely will attract college business with this promotion. But you'll benefit even if your sign didn't appear to bring in any young people. Anyone passing by your window and seeing your sign (or seeing your small newspaper ad) will get the subliminal message that your salon is capable of precision work, and you care about delivering to the customer exactly what she wants. When a nonclient gets that message about your salon, it may indeed influence her when she thinks she may be ready for a perm or color. If she has any fears at all about any new service she hasn't tried, your Guaranteed Haircut message will encourage her to use your salon. People want to be assured and reassured that they'll get what they ask for and that stylists will be sensitive to their beauty desires.

Client Rewards
& Coupons

Reward Clients with a Sign-Up Bonus

In the "old days," which a lot of folks nowadays don't remember, clients would have "standing" appointments. They'd come in every week at the same time for the same service, usually a "Wash 'n Set." Those days are long gone. Nowadays a client finishes her appointment, waves good-bye, and calls for her next appointment when the spirit moves her. It doesn't positively, absolutely have to be that way. You can encourage people to not necessarily make a week-in, week-out standing appointment but at least make their next appointment.

If a client has just had a perm, you know that she'll need another in maybe three months. Why not encourage her to sign up for it right now? If she's a haircut client, you know she ought to be coming back in four to six weeks. Let's get her signed up right now.

1 One way to do this is to offer a reward for signing up for the next appointment when you're finished with the current appointment. The very first thing you must do is to train whoever collects clients' money on the way out to ask if she'd like to make her next appointment and thus qualify for the "Sign-up Bonus." Everyone has to be asked, no exceptions.

2 Then you need a big sign in the area that says:

SIGN-UP BONUS
Schedule your next appointment before you leave.
When you come in, we'll have a special gift for you:
a FREE "Paraffin Wax Treatment."

I noted that the reward would be "a free paraffin wax treatment" because I saw that in a salon that was employing this promotional idea. Obviously you can offer any reward you'd like. It can be a free five to ten minute scalp massage, a conditioning treatment, a retail hair care product, a nail care service, or whatever you'd like.

OFFER A REWARD FOR SIGNING UP FOR THE NEXT APPOINTMENT WHEN YOU'RE FINISHED WITH THE CURRENT APPOINTMENT.

NOTES

Most clients will sign up for their next appointment to qualify for the reward. Why not? They have nothing to lose and everything to gain. If they want to cancel the appointment, they certainly can do so. But if they keep it, they get your free little goodie.

But scheduling the appointment is not enough to assure that they'll show up. You've got to remind them, as well. A week before the appointment you should send out a reminder card. An even better idea is to call them to "confirm."

When they do show up for that appointment, give them their reward eagerly and happily. It means that in the weeks or months since you saw them last, they have been exposed to all sorts of temptations to visit other salons, but your device of having them make that advance appointment, rewarding them for it, and reminding them of it, has paid off. They're back in your salon.

And when they leave, it's "Here-we-go-again time." We start the whole procedure all over again.

Build Your Unisex Business by Attracting Couples

CLIENT REWARD

Can you remember the time when absolutely *no* men ever patronized salons? They went to barbershops. Some patronized "barber stylists." None patronized "beauty parlors." That was a couple of decades ago, but there are still many men who don't get their hair cut in salons. Often it doesn't even occur to them. Or they may feel awkward walking into a salon and scheduling an appointment. These guys have to be taken by the hand and led in. Who better to lead them in but the women in their lives—their wives, their girlfriends, sometimes even their mothers.

It's often the case that a woman who likes the way her hair gets cut in her favorite salon may wish that her husband or boyfriend would get it cut there, too. She may think her haircut is better executed than his. Does she say anything to him about it? Usually not. That's a private territory, and she's reluctant to intrude. You've got to give her a reason. What better reason can there be than the one word that will always attract her attention: Discount! Now, then . . .

1 If you want to keep costs down, you don't even have to spend any money at all publicizing this one. No newspaper ads, no postcards, no signs, no buttons. Just each stylist saying to each female client:

"Can I tell you something? Next month we're having a special promotion for *couples*. When you book your next appointment, if you also book an appointment at the very same time for your husband [or boyfriend or son or whomever], he gets his cut at fifty percent off."

2 If you'd like, you can really go crazy and offer the man's haircut for free. That, in effect, will be two haircuts for the price of one. That means the client's cut is actually discounted 50 percent. Who can resist this kind of bargain? The amount of the discount is of course up to you. But why not be generous? After all, it's not a promotion that's going to last forever. You'll only run it for a month, maybe two. The object is to attract male clients and to beef up your unisex business. A free haircut or beefy

A FREE HAIRCUT OR BEEFY DISCOUNT WILL ATTRACT MEN YOU HAVEN'T BEEN ABLE TO LURE INTO THE SALON FOR ALL THESE YEARS.

discount will attract men you haven't been able to lure into the salon for all these years. Now you'll have them!

Then, too, it's kind of a social situation. If the husband comes in with the wife, chances are that when they leave they'll go out to dinner. So that's a night out they might not normally have had. Boyfriend-girlfriend? You've got to admit, it's a very different kind of date—different enough so that they'll both probably enjoy it. Yes, you'll be giving away a lot of free or discounted haircuts, but if some of those guys like the way they're treated, like the results, and elect to have their hair cut regularly in your salon, you'll be way ahead of the game.

Referral
Cards

Everyone knows that the best advertising is word-of-mouth referrals. What could be better than a satisfied client extolling your virtues to a friend? What referral cards do is push the process along a little. It reminds clients to recommend you just in case it slips their minds. And as an added push, it gives clients an incentive to pass the word along. You can give each of your clients a referral card to recommend friends with, but let's try to go that idea one better.

CLIENT REWARD

WHAT COULD BE BETTER
THAN A SATISFIED
CLIENT EXTOLLING YOUR
VIRTUES TO A FRIEND?

1 Give the client *five* referral cards held together with a small rubberband. The differences between five cards and one card are formidable.

- Five cards are much less likely to be lost, discarded, or mixed in with an assortment of the miscellaneous debris that can accumulate in a handbag or drawer.

- Five cards subtly suggest to the client that you expect, or at least hope, that she will refer you to several of her friends, not just one.

- You may not see the client for a couple of months. During that time she will interact with many of her friends. If she goes to lunch with a group and she only has one card, the opportunity will be missed to spread the word among the others.

2 What should the card say? I've seen many, many different messages. Here is one suggestion. You can use it, or change it, or discard it, or communicate the thought in any way you'd like.

This card entitles the bearer to a
FREE
**Deep Conditioning Treatment (Value $10)
and in conjunction with any other service
available in the salon. To a Friend Of**

_____

**from Margie's Hair Salon
333 Main Street
Oak Park, Kansas
234-5678**

BE LIBERAL WITH THE

INCENTIVE AND

EXTRAORDINARILY

SOLICITOUS AND

PROFESSIONAL IN

MAKING THAT FIRST

IMPRESSION.

3 Obviously, you can make any services available as the incentive. A manicure is always attractive; so is the thought of a ten to fifteen-minute scalp massage. Conditioning is usually appropriate because virtually everyone can use it. Don't be fussy about whatever service it is the friend would like to qualify for the free treatment. The object of the referral card is to bring someone into the salon who has not been there before. Once she's there, you're on display, you're auditioning, you've got a shot. If she becomes a regular client, she'll spend hundreds of dollars in your salon. The point is to be liberal with the incentive and extraordinarily solicitous and professional in making that first impression.

4 When any of these referrals comes in, it's critically important to remember the client who got her to come in. Your incentive offer to the new client should be duplicated with an identical incentive offer to the existing client. In other words, the client who refers her friends should also get a free conditioning treatment or manicure or scalp massage or what-have-you for each client she refers. Tell that to each client as you give them their little packet of five rubberbanded referral cards.

5 On the very day that a new client comes in for an appointment, or at the latest the next day, the referring client should be called, hopefully by you the owner of the salon or by the manager. She should be thanked and told that on her next appointment, she'll be scheduled for that additional free service. This thank-you call will also serve to remind her to make an appointment. In most cases she'll do it right then during the thank-you call.

The possibilities of increased business with the referral cards are mind-boggling. If each of your clients referred only one friend, that would double your business. And you're not asking them to recommend one friend, you're asking for five. The possibilities of dramatically increased business are so attractive that you should make the "appreciation service" as generous as possible. It *will* pay off.

"Fast Beauty"— For Women in a Hurry

CLIENT REWARD

ABSOLUTELY GUARANTEE
TO GET A WOMAN IN
AND OUT OF THE SALON
WITHIN AN HOUR.

Women can't be categorized anymore. We can't just say they are "career women" or "housewives" or any other designation. Nowadays there are so many variations of every way of life.

However, one element of life *is* common to virtually all women, whether housewife, executive, salesperson, soccer mom, or astronaut, which is that they simply don't have enough hours in the day. Indeed we often hear a woman say, "I just don't have time to go to a salon." She may be right or she may be wrong about that. If a salon visit means not being taken exactly on time and having a total visit that takes two or three hours, she's right. She just can't spare that time. She may not even be able to give herself that time in an evening or on weekends. But how about if we could absolutely guarantee to get her in and out within an hour? She generally *can* take that amount of time out from her schedule, and she probably knows she needs and wants to. Let's go attract these women.

1 Determine what services you can positively deliver in an hour or less. Shampoo? Cut? Style? Blowout? If you can't combine all of those and complete them within sixty minutes from "Hello" to "Good-bye" something's wrong. You've got to work on it. You've got to practice, have training sessions, clinics. Get every segment down to a certain number of minutes so that it all totals less than sixty.

2 Nail services. Certainly while the hair is being worked on, the client's nails can be worked on. In many salons hair and nails are two separate services done at two separate times. In many others, however, the services are combined. No reason why they can't be or shouldn't be.

3 Haircoloring. This is a tougher one. Some haircoloring services simply can't be done in an hour. You can't take a client with very dark hair who wants to be very light haired and do the whole job in a limited period of time. That's unrealistic. Clients don't even expect it. But there are many other services, including glazing, mini-highlighting, and color brightening, that can be done relatively quickly and even combined with styling services to get women out quickly.

4 Go through every one of your services, and determine which you can do when seconds and minutes are precious to the client—and the revenue to be gained is precious to you.

5 Now you've got to get the word out. If you're in a downtown business area, print up a flyer describing your "Fast Beauty" services, and have them given out right on the street. Don't consider it beneath your dignity. All kinds of cards, flyers, and ads are distributed in busy downtown areas. No reason why you should be left out. It will bring in business.

6 If you're in a suburban or rural area with not a lot of offices and business people, be assured there are still plenty of busy people around. Distribute small descriptive brochures on what you can offer in a one-hour period.

7 Make sure you always emphasize "Your appointment will always start exactly on time, and you will be out and on your way in sixty minutes or less."

8 Ask clients to specify they want the "Fast Beauty treatment" when they book their appointments. That way you'll know that you have to have the decks cleared so the client is taken the minute she walks in. If she's a Fast Beauty client, you wouldn't book a permanent wave or corrective color job immediately before her appointment with the operator who's supposed to work on her. Some common sense and careful scheduling is called for here.

DON'T GET SO CAUGHT UP IN THE QUICK-SERVICE THING THAT YOU START RUSHING EVERYBODY.

9 Remember, too, that the client in a rush is only one type of client. Other clients want to come in, relax, luxuriate, and be pampered. Don't get so caught up in the quick-service thing that you start rushing everybody. You *can* be all things to all people. You *can* get the busy woman in and out in an hour, and you *can* provide a relaxing experience for the woman who has the luxury of doing so.

In case you're thinking that you're asking your salon to be schizophrenic, don't sweat it. Have you ever gone into a restaurant and told the maître d' that you're in a hurry or you have to make a plane or you've got to get in and out by a certain time? They accommodate. They take your order quicker, they give it to the chef quicker, they serve it quicker and they present your bill quicker. This happens all the time. You can do it, and the client on the go will love you for it.

You Can't Fix Anything Till You Know What's Broke

CLIENT REWARD

IF YOU CAN GET AN ACCURATE AND IMPARTIAL ASSESSMENT OF YOUR SALON OPERATION, IT WILL HELP YOU ENORMOUSLY.

One of the most difficult tasks a salon owner has is to get completely objective evaluations of the salon and its operations. You can't do it yourself, you're too close. Friends can't do it; they're too close to you. And yet it's extremely important. You try very hard. You think you're doing all the right things. But when a complete stranger comes in, she gets a total first impression that you can't possibly experience yourself. Things can be happening in sights, sounds, and smells that can directly impact your business both positively and negatively. You can spot some of them, but a brand-new set of eyes, ears, and sensitivities will unearth more. It's vital for you to have this kind of information so that you can enhance what's good and correct what isn't. If you can get an accurate and impartial assessment of your salon operation, it will help you enormously. And it's very easy to do.

1. In the course of your business and social activities *outside* the salon, you meet many women (and men) of various ages and accomplishments. When you do meet someone a) who works or lives reasonably close to the salon and b) is the kind of person you'd like to have as a client, you "make them an offer they can't refuse."

2. Here's the proposition you offer. You say:

    Make an appointment for services in my salon any time you'd like. Schedule yourself for any service we have. Pay whatever the charges are. Tip whatever you'd like. Then write me a *detailed report* telling me all of your impressions, good and bad. What were your first impressions? How were you greeted? Were you treated professionally? Were you pleased with the services performed? Was the salon clean? Do you have suggestions that would improve your experience? And so on. As soon as I receive your report, I'll send you a check completely reimbursing you for your outlay.

3 Whom you pick for this mission is up to you, and since you'll be using your own good judgment, it's improbable that anyone will abuse your generosity by lavishly tipping or using too many services. Do this exercise on a regular basis, *at least* half a dozen times a year.

4 The information you receive will be invaluable. You may be used to some of the smells but learn that it can turn people off. You may think your bathroom is clean enough, but it may be not so to a client. You may like the music you have playing in the background, but it may be an annoyance to others. You may think it's cool, permissive, and liberal to have your stylists wear jeans, sweatshirts, and sneakers. Others may find it unprofessional. The list is endless. Strangers will see things that you're absolutely oblivious to.

5 When evaluations start coming in, take steps to remedy anything that is negative. If you're uncertain whether a specific criticism is valid, wait until you get the next evaluation or two. If it comes up again, it's definitely a red flag. Fix it.

6 As soon as you get the letter/report from your evaluator, call her up and thank her. Then probe a bit more to dig wider and deeper about the problem areas. Then thank her again.

EACH TIME A PROBLEM AREA IS IDENTIFIED AND REMEDIED, YOU MAKE THE SALON EXPERIENCE MORE PLEASURABLE.

7 Each time a problem area is identified and remedied, you make the salon experience more pleasurable. In the course of many months and many reports you will inevitably improve your client retention rate and get more word-of-mouth recommendations than has historically been the case. The salon experience should be a *totally* pleasant and positive one. If it is, people will keep coming back. If it isn't, if some little thing annoys them, they'll be ripe pickings for a competitor whom they feel may provide the same service but without the negative annoyance(s).

Remember this *is* a promotion. It's not one that will have clients breaking down your door, but it *is* one that will result in increased business—and that's what a good promotion should do.

Now here's a bonus. People love personal attention. They like having an "inside track." Each person you ask to be an evaluator will like the idea, the opportunity, the free services, and the personal attention and expression of appreciation from you. Nine times out of ten, maybe ten times out of ten, they'll become regular clients of your salon. And won't that be great? You get all this valuable information and you get new clients. No mailing lists, no signs, no advertising, no delays. You can get going on this one today.

Turning Raffles into Rewards

CLIENT REWARD

Every one of your clients belongs to at least one organization, usually more. And doesn't it sometimes seem as though each of these organizations runs a raffle sometime during the year? What a bore and what a chore. When a client asks you to buy a raffle ticket, it's hard to say no. And that's not the end of it. As if it isn't bad enough that you feel obliged to buy one raffle ticket, clients often expect you to buy a whole book! They reason that since they're spending a few hundred dollars in your salon over the course of a year, the least you can do is spend $25 to $50 on their organization.

If this is a serious problem with you and your clientele, you can eliminate it on the one hand and build business on the other. The idea is to substitute a prize as your donation to the organization instead of buying a batch of raffle tickets. Here's how you go about it.

1 Put up a discreet sign somewhere in your reception area saying:

SPECIAL COURTESY TO THELMA & LOUISE CLIENTS

**If you belong to an organization that plans on having
a raffle program, please let us know. We will be happy
to participate by donating a prize.**

2 The prize you donate is, of course, totally up to you. What usually makes an impression is "A Day of Beauty." The prize can consist of anything you feel might be appropriate. Usually it would contain such things as shampoo, cut, restyle, blowout, manicure, facial treatment, and makeup. If that's a little too rich for you, extract any services you'd like. Want to enrich it? Maybe add waxing, scalp massage, or color highlighting.

3 It doesn't end there. When the client asks you for the donation of the prize, tell her that some "provisions" do apply.

• It is an absolute that the name of your salon must appear on all raffle literature.

- Request that you be one of those who will pick the winning tickets.
- If the kick-off of the raffle program is at one of the organization's meetings, ask to be present so that everyone can know who you are and how generous you are.
- If the winners are picked at an organization function, by all means ask to be present so that your generosity can be acknowledged.
- You may specify days on which the prize can be claimed. Surely you won't want to do a complimentary Day of Beauty on a busy weekend. Since "the price is right," winners will be happy to come in during a time convenient for the salon.

4 When the winner has claimed her prize, make sure to take a photo of the finished product with the appropriate stylist gazing on it admiringly. The photo can be sent to the organization for use in any publication that it may put out. It can also be sent to local newspapers that often like to get pictures of local people and organizations into its stories. You can work directly with the publicity chairperson (if it has one) to help you get this newspaper coverage. After all, it will help publicize the organization, too.

What does all this accomplish? Let's take your donation of A Day of Beauty to just one organization.

WILL ALL THIS EXPOSURE AND APPRECIATION RESULT IN INCREASED BUSINESS? IT CAN'T MISS.

- By virtue of appearing on the raffle and other organization literature, the name of your salon and your gift will be made familiar to hundreds of people.
- If you appear at any of the organization functions, you'll meet still more people who will be appreciative of your generosity.
- If you get publicity in a local newspaper, still more people will be exposed to you and your salon's name.
- The winner of the Day of Beauty may very well become a salon client.
- You won't have to buy a book of raffle tickets from the client who represents this organization.

Those are the benefits from the donation of a prize to only one organization. If you do this with a dozen organizations, multiply those benefits by twelve. Now we're *really* talking about a lot of people who get exposed to your name and the name of your salon. A lot of people who will appreciate your generosity and your community spirit.

Will all this exposure and appreciation result in increased business? It can't miss.

A Kiss Says
Thank You

One of the most satisfying moments in the operation of a salon is when someone calls for an appointment and says she was recommended by another client. It's affirmation that you've done your job well—so well that a client has told a friend to entrust her beauty needs to you. Isn't that wonderful?

Some salons try to encourage clients to recommend people and offer various incentives. That's all right, and there are many salons that have used this incentive-type promotion for many years. It's a little "obvious," however. In effect, you're "bribing" clients to push your salon so they can get the reward. If it works, fine, but a more subtle approach might be better—and classier in the long run. Instead of offering clients an incentive to recommend their friends, why not thank them in a very lovely way *after* they have recommended their friends without the thought of a reward? Try this approach as a substitute for the "bribe."

CLIENT REWARD

PRINTED MATERIAL

1 A kiss is a wonderful expression of appreciation so let's have an imprint of a "thank-you kiss" printed on a card.

2 Use copy something along these lines:

[Name] recently visited us as a result of your recommendation.

Thank you very much. We're very happy that both you and your friend have enjoyed our services. Please accept this "kiss" as a token of our appreciation, and bring this card with you on your next appointment. We'll be happy to deduct 10 percent from all your service and product charges.

Thanks again. We look forward to seeing you soon so that we can thank you in person.

Color 'N Comb • 103 Plaza Street • Centerville •
Tel. 692–2966

When the client gets this card, it will come as a complete surprise, and she'll be absolutely delighted. Her reaction will be, "Isn't that nice of them?" and she will surely be motivated to recommend others.

3 The whole process will be appropriately completed when she comes in again and you indeed approach her and happily thank her for her referral. It's important that whoever does the salon's booking has a complete listing of all clients who have received these "kiss" cards. When a client calls for an appointment, you, as the owner of the salon, should be notified as should the stylist working on her so that both of you can thank her. She will appreciate that.

In a world where good deeds and kindnesses often go unnoticed, your expressions of appreciation will be like flowers in a desert, and they will have a way of building on themselves. Clients who receive these cards will be favorably inclined toward your salon and will consequently recommend even more clients. This in turn will prompt more appreciative expressions from you, which will yet again result in more clients. What a lovely way to build a business.

Use Discount Coupons to Build up Business

We are surround by coupons. The Sunday papers are full of them, they come in fat envelopes in the mail, they are given out at supermarkets. Know why they're so all-pervasive? Because they work! You may even collect them yourself. You know that when you're shopping, if you have a coupon for anything you need, you'll pay less. But coupons encourage another phenomenon. If the discount is strong enough, you may, in fact, buy something that wouldn't normally be on your shopping list. People just can't resist a good deal. Let's put that coupon philosophy to work for you.

No doubt some facet of your business isn't as strong as you'd like it to be. Maybe it's nail services. You see nail salons heavily booked while few of your clients have their nails done. Or you lament that perms are down, and you want to encourage people into that service again. Whatever it is that can use some building, coupons can help you build it. Here's how.

COUPON

PEOPLE CAN'T RESIST A GOOD BUY. PUT THE COUPON PHILOSOPHY TO WORK FOR YOU.

1 Have your local printer print coupons the size of a dollar bill. Place a value on each coupon of, let's say, $1. Obviously that amount can vary. You can make the value of the coupon 50¢ or $1.50 or $3 or whatever. On every visit to your salon, each client receives this coupon on the way out.

2 Keep your coupons completely transferable so that if one client has a few and elects to give hers to her mother or a friend, by all means allow it. If they're talking about you and collecting coupons and swapping and exchanging, it will all result in more appointments, more business.

3 It should say very clearly on the coupon that it may be redeemed toward the specific service that you want to build up and encourage. You don't have to use this exact copy, but you can say something like:

This coupon is worth $1 when the bearer redeems it toward the payment of any nail service.

Signed:

For New Images Studio

4 It's a nice idea to personalize each of the coupons by signing each one of them yourself and in a different color ink than the print on the coupon. (This will also discourage anyone from even thinking of duplicating the coupon and forging your signature.)

5 Some of your clients won't bother to use the coupons. It will mean nothing to them. Don't worry about it. After all, many people do their shopping without any coupons. On the other hand, we've all seen the ladies in the supermarket with an envelope jammed full of them. You'll get the same kind of percentages. Some will use them, some won't. But if you have a client who gets her nails done elsewhere because it's a dollar or two cheaper, this coupon will automatically level the playing field and give her the incentive to have her nails done with you.

Other client may be savers. They'll save up $5 to $10 worth of coupons so that they can get a significant discount for a comprehensive nail service.

6 If it's a service like perms that you want to encourage, the $1 coupon may not be enough of an incentive. If you charge, say $50 or more for a perm, you may want to offer as much as a $5 coupon. Once a client has two or three of those in her possession, she'll think very seriously about booking a perm appointment. And if she does book, and she is happy with the result, you've got yourself a new perm client who'll schedule herself for anywhere from two to four perms a year. That will be well worth your coupon investment.

7 Skin care is another service that often needs encouragement. Skin care service in salons usually builds very slowly. Anything you can do to help it along will positively pay off in the long run. Be generous with skin care coupons.

This is a very flexible device. You can even use it to get clients to cut their hair more often, or to sign up for a specific kind of haircoloring service.

Everyone loves a bargain. Your coupons will give it to them—and bring in a lot of plus business.

EVERYONE LOVES A BAR-
GAIN. YOUR COUPONS
WILL GIVE IT TO THEM—
AND BRING IN A LOT OF
PLUS BUSINESS.

Go After
Former Clients

COUPON

PRINTED MATERIAL

Wouldn't it be wonderful if every client who walked into the salon became a permanent client, scheduling appointments every month or two forever? Every year you'd need more real estate to accommodate them.

Regrettably, the real world doesn't work that way. Most people do stay on board, a good many don't. Many salon owners reason that if a client doesn't show up for a few months, she was probably unhappy with a service or treatment she received, or she elected to try a new salon for whatever reason, she moved, she died, or all of the above. But it's a mistake to give up on a former client. There really are dozens of possible reasons why she hasn't come around. Who knows what they all are? We do know that everyone likes to be "wooed," so why don't we woo her?

WE KNOW THAT
EVERYONE LIKES TO BE
"WOOED," SO LET'S
WOO THOSE FORMER
CLIENTS BACK.

1 Go through your records, and see who hasn't had an appointment in the last six months. Accumulate the list, and then go out and buy a batch of postcards, one for each name on the list. As of this writing, postcards cost 20¢ to mail. That's a wonderfully economical way to make contact.

2 The cards can convey any message you feel would be attractive and provide an incentive for clients to call. As a suggestion let's try:

WE MISS YOU!

We haven't seen you here at the Ultima Salon for quite a while. During this time we've added some wonderfully creative hairstylists, and we've all been steadily attending classes, seminars, clinics, and workshops in every phase of the beauty arts. All so that we can offer our clients the very best and latest in cutting, conditioning, coloring, perming, skin care, and nail care. We invite you to call for an appointment soon. When you come in please bring this card with you. We'll be delighted to . . .

NOTES

DEDUCT 10 PERCENT ON ALL OUR SERVICES AND RETAIL PRODUCTS.

We are looking forward to seeing you soon.

ULTIMA SALON • 333 North Street • Centerville • Tel. 992-8534

Take that card to the printer, and ask him to help you with the choice of typefaces and layout. If you'd like, have somebody who has a lovely handwriting actually write the message out so that it looks like a personal card from a friend.

When the client comes back, she's giving you another chance. Make the most of it. If she likes what she gets, and she feels at home, you've wooed her and won her back.

This is not a one-time promotion. It should be ongoing. Every three months or so send another set of postcards, another message in the same vein, another incentive. Every time you do a mailing, you'll get a positive response from a certain percentage of the recipients. The first couple of appointments will pay for the mailing. After that it's all gravy.

Winston Churchill once said that the most important message he could possibly convey to people was contained in seven words: "Never, never, never, never, never give up." If those words and that message could help Great Britain to victory in World War II, they'll help you with former clients.

Start a Frequent Beautifier Club

COUPON

Do you belong to any of the airlines' frequent-flyer clubs? If you travel, you do. Everyone who travels belongs. Many salons have adopted variations of the basic idea, and if your plan is soundly crafted, it will build your business. You can call your promotion a "Frequent Beautifier Club," or just have it as the Name-of-Your-Salon Club. Here are some suggestions that will help you get it going.

1. Send every client on your mailing list a letter, automatically enrolling them in your Frequent Beautifier Club. Whatever number of dollars a client spends in your salon, that's the number of points she'll get on each visit. Points can be accrued toward services and/or retail products. When clients spend, they get points.

2. If you're computerized, enter the number of points into your database for each client. If you aren't computerized, set up a card system whereby you record how many dollars they spent, and therefore how many points they have earned, on each visit.

3. Determine what the benefits are that they'll receive at various point levels. It's a good idea to focus the redemptions on services you're trying to build. If, for example, you're satisfied with the amount of cuts and colors you do but would like to do more in the area of skin care, massage, waxing, or manicures, those are the services that should be available at various redemption levels.

4. Practically everyone on your staff will, at one time or another, be the ones performing the "free" services. They must all understand that while they won't be earning commissions on these services, they'll actually be building their clientele and will, of course, receive appropriate tips.

5. How generous or frugal should you be? That's really up to you, but a good number to work with is 10 percent. When a client spends $100 and therefore accumulates 100 points, she'll be entitled, for example, to a free manicure worth approximately $10. Obviously the more generous you are, the more enthusiastic your client participants will be.

WHATEVER NUMBER OF DOLLARS A CLIENT SPENDS IN YOUR SALON, THAT'S THE NUMBER OF POINTS SHE'LL GET ON EACH VISIT.

6 Take another tip from the airlines, and give extra-generous rewards to your top-spending clients. Just as the airlines have silver and gold memberships, you can do the same. The more you flatter clients, the more you'll encourage their patronage, and the more loyalty you'll engender.

7 Keep this in mind: You will never get 100 percent redemption, so if you offer services that amount to 10 percent you'll actually be redeeming somewhere around 7 to 8 percent. Therefore, if you can afford the 10 percent figures, you can actually offer something closer to 15 percent knowing that the "lost" redemptions will bring the real overall figure down to 10 percent. There will always be people who relocate or stop coming to the salon for one reason or another, and those points simply won't be redeemed.

8 You want your clients to actively participate in this program and always be aware of what their point level is. You know that when you belong to a Frequent Flyer Club the airline generally keeps you updated monthly. You don't have to do it that frequently, but you certainly ought to send out a quarterly mailing that tells all clients how many points they have accumulated. Always reiterate all the benefits and services that are available at various point levels.

9 When each client leaves the salon, she should be given a card indicating how many points she has accumulated. This simple device will encourage and motivate some clients to book their next appointment on the spot.

10 Try to set up a system on your computer or otherwise whereby when the client calls for an appointment, you can instantly access the number of points she has accumulated. When you inform her of the level she's at, she may elect to book an extra service or two just to boost her point level to the next plateau so that she'll qualify for the particular service she'd like.

You'll find that clients will enjoy your Frequent Beautifier Club as thoroughly and enthusiastically as they enjoy accumulating points with the airlines. It will become routine after a while to want to accumulate more points and be eligible for more benefits. In addition to the incentive that will help build the tabs on each visit, you'll be getting the additional benefit of communicating with clients more often than you ordinarily would. The quarterly point-update statements will be reminders for them to come in. You'll also be able to include other information as inserts in the mailing— and that will be still *more* communicating.

"Mad Money" Is Irresistible

The American consumer—me and doubtlessly you included—simply can't resist bargains. Look at any issue of the Sunday papers. There are always inserts containing dozens of coupons redeemable with dozens of products. This is big business and it works. Haven't you seen women in the supermarket with purses, wallets, or envelopes filled with coupons? Often if the incentive is good enough people will actually purchase products they didn't intend to, just to get the bargain price. That's the reason manufacturers invest in these coupon promotions. If the consumers can be induced into buying a product because of the bargain price, they may purchase the product again when their supply is low, this time at regular prices. It works for manufacturers, it can work for you.

You can use this device to promote any service at all. If too small a percentage of your clientele is having their hair colored in your salon, you can use it to promote haircolor. If you've just hired someone who's an accomplished waxing person, by all means use it to promote waxing. You can even use it to promote one specific stylist, perhaps a new employee, in the salon. Here's how to go about it.

COUPON

YOU CAN USE THIS DEVICE TO PROMOTE ANY SERVICE AT ALL.

1 Have a coupon printed up, representing a $5 bill (obviously if you don't like this figure, you can raise or lower it to any dollar amount you want). Print the coupons on some sort of green paper stock so that it evokes the idea of real money, "greenbacks." The size can be anything you feel would be convenient, from as small as your business card to as large as a standard dollar bill or even larger. Your printer will be able to advise you on what the cheapest size would be.

2 Let's title the coupon "Mad Manicure Money." Or it can be "Mad Waxing Money," "Mad Haircolor Money," or "Mad" anything. If you don't like the word "Mad," pick a word you *do* like—perhaps "Perm Pin Money" or "Wild Waxing Money" or "Mini Makeover Money." You're the promoter, you're the creative person. Give it some thought to come up with exactly the right words, words you'll feel comfortable with.

3 Under the headline, say something like: This $5 bill is fully redeemable toward any nail service (or haircolor or waxing service).

4 You may also want to include an expiration date. Almost every coupon you'll ever see has such a date. It gets people to use the coupon sooner rather than later. It's also a good idea to have an authorization signature. Use your actual signature in a colored ink. With computer printing and color duplicating services being so readily available these days, there's always a possibility, though small, that someone can duplicate your "Mad Money." Having an actual and recognizable signature will discourage fraud.

5 In the center of the "bill," in the space normally devoted to a presidential picture on standard currency, insert your salon logo or a photo of a model representing the service you're promoting—or your own photo. If you have employed a new stylist with no following, you can put the stylist's photo in this area and have him/her give out these coupons at nearby shopping areas or local merchants. Handing a few hundred of these to strangers will jump-start the building of a new clientele.

6 Normally these coupons would be given to existing clients with each appointment. Give it to them when they come in the door rather than when they pay their bill. This will encourage them to avail themselves right now of the service you are promoting.

7 After about two or three months change the promotion so that you'll be encouraging clients to avail themselves of yet another service.

This promotion can go on all year long. If you change it every two to three months you'll be encouraging clients to take advantage of significant discounts on four to six different salon services during the course of the year. Surely you have many clients who don't have anything done except have their hair cut. Others may get one or two other services. But they're still not trying four to six services—and that's what this whole promotion is designed to get them to do.

You've got a full-service salon with a full menu of services. Just as a restaurant doesn't only want to sell you an entrée but also a glass of wine, salad, soup, appetizer, and dessert, so you should endeavor to have every client using multiple services. Offering this promotion on an ongoing basis will accomplish this task.

Miscellaneous Prep

Got a Scrapbook? Make It More Productive!

PREPARATION TIME

There are so many pictorial styling books around nowadays that many salons have stopped compiling their old-fashioned styling scrapbooks. That's a mistake. You *should* have one or two of these books up front in the reception/waiting area. They can supplement the commercial styling books. Who knows, in the future they can even replace them. Not only will this device not cost you anything, but you'll actually save money if you use your own styling scrapbooks instead of some of the ones they sell at shows. Of course, you may actually be using scrapbooks all along; if so, good for you. If you do, here are a few tips that can make them more productive.

1 Always keep your styling books neat and current. What could be worse than having a scrapbook that's dog-eared and features hairstyles from the Charlie's Angels era? No, go through them frequently. Remove stuff you'd rather not be doing, and put in illustrations that you're confident your salon can execute and that indicate you're absolutely up-to-the-moment. Are there styles and colors your clients should know about? Get 'em in. Are there hot new actresses and celebrities that your clients may want to emulate? Get 'em in. You can be certain that your clients would much rather look through these custom-made scrapbooks than the posed photos in the commercial styling books.

2 Don't confine your scrapbook merely to hair. Cut out photos of nails and nail art and include them. Beautiful makeup effects should go in. Have any of the retail products you carry been written about or featured in the magazines? Cut out the articles and put them in.

3 Don't just use photos in your scrapbook. If you come across a short, interesting article on *any* aspect of health or beauty, include it. The more interesting your scrapbook is, the more inclined your clients will be to spend time going through it rather than some magazines you may have lying around.

MANY SALONS HAVE STOPPED COMPILING THEIR OLD-FASHIONED STYLING SCRAPBOOKS. THAT'S A MISTAKE.

4 Now, here's the idea that will double, triple, quadruple the value of your scrapbook. Take little Post-it Notes, and write short comments on many of the photos and articles in the book. Comments like: "Bangs always emphasize the eyes;" "A wonderful style if you don't have time to fuss with your hair;" "If you want to attract attention, try this shade of nail polish;" "This style is wonderful for a round face;" or "Conditioning treatment would have tamed her frizzies." You'll doubtlessly have dozens of comments and thoughts while leafing through the pages. *Share* those thoughts with your clients. It's not hard. Try it. Your clients will love it.

5 Affix a card on the outside of your scrapbook that says UP-TO-DATE BEAUTY PHOTOS AS OF [MONTH, YEAR]. When a client sees the date, she'll know it's not the same old book she saw last year. She'll want to go through it to stay current herself. If you have the time, edit the scrapbook *monthly*. That way your "regulars" will want to go through it on each visit.

6 If you have the time and inclination, do more than one book. Do two or even more. You can label them Volume I, Volume II, and so on.

YOU CAN SPECIALIZE.

HAVE ONE BOOK

COMPLETELY DEVOTED

TO DIFFERENT STYLES,

ANOTHER DEVOTED TO

DIFFERENT HAIR COLORS

AND TECHNIQUES.

7 If you'd like, you can specialize. Have one book completely devoted to different styles, another devoted to different haircolors and techniques. You can have one strictly for nails and another strictly for makeup.

8 All of this takes time, but it's time well spent. You personally don't have to do it all. Surely there are people in the salon who would enjoy this activity and who have free time during the course of some days. Instead of sitting around doing the crossword puzzle, they can go through magazines, cutting, commenting, and inserting in your scrapbooks.

Does all this effort result in business? Better believe it!

- The scrapbooks tell your clients you're interested in them.
- The photos will suggest new styles, colors, and cuts that will mean extra services *on this visit*.
- Your comments will intrigue clients, titillate them, impress them.

Those are all pluses, and pluses translate into more business. And have you noticed? This whole idea, this entire activity, costs you only the price of the binders. This has to be a promotion you can't refuse.

Before-and-After Photos— Always a Hit

PREPARATION TIME

Every beauty editor of every women's publication knows one fact as surely as she knows the sun will rise in the East. People love to see before-and-after photos, makeover photos. Whenever they run these types of features in their publications, they know that the readership is virtually 100 percent. You're a pro, you transform people all the time, and yet when you run across one of these magazine articles, you, too, probably stop to look at it, read it, and take it all in. You can put the fascination for makeovers to work for you in attracting clients. Here are some suggestions that will help to make everyone's fascination with makeovers into a promotion.

1 As regular or new clients come in for their appointments, "recruit" some of them to be the subject of before-and-after photos. Sometimes clients themselves will request a totally new look. Sometimes you or your stylists will successfully suggest makeovers.

2 When you have a likely subject, you've got to give it time and attention. You can't just whip out your trusty Polaroid and take a quickie snapshot. You have to have a halfway decent camera and appropriate lighting. You may already own the camera. But the background and lighting take a little more knowledge. Do you know anyone who's a photography buff? Is there a local photographer in the community who will advise you in exchange for some free services? Does the local high school have a photography club?

3 Reserve some spot in your salon for the "sittings." You'll have to buy two or three special lights for eliminating shadows or emphasizing certain features. Your expenditures will actually be minimal. And remember, anything you buy will be deductible. Save your receipts.

4 When you have the suitable subject and the right photography set up, it will take only a few minutes to sit the client down, put the lights on, and take her "before" photo. When she's finished (and finished means not only hair but makeup, as well), take at least a dozen or more shots of her in the "after" mode.

YOU CAN PUT THE FASCINATION FOR MAKEOVERS TO WORK FOR YOU IN ATTRACTING CLIENTS.

5 When the film is developed, select the appropriate before-and-after shots and have them blown up to 8 × 10. When you have about half a dozen sets of these before-and-after shots, you can mount them in your window under a sign that says MAKEOVER MAGIC or BEFORE AND AFTER AT THE IMAGES SALON or SOME OF OUR HAPPY CLIENTS.

6 Keep these photos in the window for no more than a couple of weeks. A month or so later, when you've accumulated another group of photos, feature the new ones. When you take a group out of the window, you shouldn't discard them. Mount them on a wall in the salon. Over the months the wall will be filled with these photos and will be the object of ongoing fascination by new and existing clients.

7 If you don't have an appropriate window in your salon, you can still use the before-and-after photo device in advertising, flyers, and postcards. As an inexpensive method of reproducing color photos you can have color Xeroxes made. But black and white reproductions can be even more dramatic looking than color.

8 Reduce the photos and use them in mailings. Can you imagine someone receiving a sheet of a dozen or so makeover photos under the headline WE DO MAKEOVER MAGIC EVERY DAY AT THE GUYS AND DOLLS SALON—COME IN FOR A FREE CONSULTATION. No one will toss that mailing away. They'll go through it head by head, first to see if there's anyone in the photos they know and then to see if any of the hairstyles would be suitable for them.

9 Whenever you do use a client's photo, it would be gracious to thank them by giving them one or more copies of the photos you've used, plus perhaps an item or two of retail hair care products you know they'd enjoy.

YOU, YOUR STYLISTS, AND YOUR CLIENTS WILL HAVE A LOT OF FUN WITH THIS ACTIVITY.

We know that clients can be fickle and can be receptive to trying a new salon if the mood hits them. If they get into this mood and they have been exposed to before-and-after images from your salon over the course of a few months, it is *your* salon that will come to mind when they're ready for the change. Their thought process will be, "I think I'm ready for a new look, and the people at that salon seem to know how to do it. They may even put my picture in their window."

All in all, you, your stylists, and your clients will have a lot of fun with this activity. Your reputation will climb, and your business will do likewise. Not a bad combination.

Try Home Hair Care Seminars

Most women get most of the information they know about hair from fashion magazines and newspapers. The publications know that all women are hungry for hair information. What is hair? How does it grow? Where does it come from? What are the problems? What are the solutions? What is the latest information? And on and on and on. There's no end to the average woman's desire for more information about hair. The editors know it, and they play right into that desire by continually scrounging up more information and passing it along. But your clients should be getting their information from *you*, shouldn't they? Then when they read about something or other in a magazine, they'll think, "I already know that. My stylist told me about it."

Sadly, many of your days go by with so many other considerations, so many other things on your mind, that the knowledge you have and should be imparting to your clients remains within you, unimparted. Don't feel too guilty; you're in very good company—but you ought to do something about it.

If it is unrealistic to think that you're going to be passing hair care information along to each of your clients on each of their appointments, consider instead hair care seminars. Here are some things to consider:

> YOUR CLIENTS SHOULD BE GETTING THEIR HAIR CARE INFORMATION FROM YOU, NOT FROM MAGAZINES.

1. Seminars can be held right in your salon at times when your salon is normally closed. Sometime in the evening would be one obvious choice; sometime during the day on a Monday would be another.

2. You should schedule these seminars for about two hours each, maybe even an hour and a half. If you run a good program and people are interested and feel they still need more information, be assured that they'll hang around when the seminar is over. What you want to avoid like the plague is dragging a program on for three hours or more so that people start looking at their watches, fidgeting, and slowly drifting away. No, shorter is better than longer.

3 You can't possibly impart everything you know in a two hour period. That's obvious. Even if you could, the audience couldn't absorb it. Instead, pick one subject. It can be on keeping haircolor fresh between visits, maintaining the look of a style between visits, or the proper way to use appliances like blowers, diffusers, and curling irons.

4 Before you do the first seminar, get a general feel for the kind of information an audience would like to have. A simple question you and your stylists can casually ask each client might be, "If you could have more knowledge and expertise on anything at all regarding your hair, what would it be?" They'll think about it a moment, and they'll tell you. No one is going to say, "I know everything I need to know. I don't need any more information." Gather your answers and impressions, and set up your programs accordingly.

YOUR SEMINARS ARE

A PUBLIC SERVICE

FOR YOUR CLIENTELE

AND FOR THE WOMEN

OF THE COMMUNITY

IN GENERAL.

5 Obviously, you can't accommodate your entire clientele in your salon. When you decide on your subject, post a sign in your window, put another sign at your reception area, and spread the word verbally through your staff. Emphasize that attendance is limited and by reservation. Note that attendees need not be clients of the salon. Your seminars are a public service for your clientele and for the women of the community in general.

6 At the seminar itself, do a little bit of talking and a lot of demonstrating. Clients see things happening in your salon all the time, but they don't know exactly what is going on. This will be their chance to sit, observe, learn, and ask questions.

7 Always book your models in advance for whatever the subject of the seminar is. Don't wait to get your models out of the audience. You may not get the right types of hair for the kind of information you want to convey.

8 Have as many of your stylists as possible doing the demos. You want to expose the talents of your group as broadly as you can. You never know exactly what and who various people in the audience will be drawn to. The more people whose talents you can expose, the better off you'll all be.

9 Keep control of the crowd. Have one person be the MC. That person can be you, or it can be one of your staff with a talent for communication. Yes, various members of the staff can answer questions on the activities they're pursuing. But the control, the flow of the events, should be in the hands of one person.

10 The time will fly by. When you officially adjourn there'll be unanswered questions. Those folks can stay, mill about, and get these questions answered.

11 Give a small gift to everyone in the audience. It can be a retail product you're interested in sampling—how much can it cost to give these gifts to perhaps a couple of dozen women?—or it can be a discount card of some sort for any of the services specifically discussed at the seminar.

You can't lose. If most of the women who attend are clients of the salon, they *will* be appreciative of the information they've received, and they *will* be impressed. If a certain percentage of the attendees are not clients of the salon, they will be equally appreciative, equally impressed, and surely will become clients when they next need the services you've discussed.

Once you do one or two of these, you'll really get the hang of it in knowing exactly how long they should last, how the room should be set up, and how you should get the word out. Your sessions will get better and better, and your bank account will do likewise.

Reminders Build Business

PREPARATION TIME

THE SOLUTION

TO FORGETFUL,

PROCRASTINATING

CLIENTS IS SENDING

OUT REMINDERS.

It would be nice if every client who came into your salon came back regularly for services every two weeks or three weeks or four. Or in the case of some other services—perms for example—every two months. But it just doesn't work out that way. Clients' schedules are crowded with their careers, their children, social obligations, and dozens of other things that cause them to forget, delay, put off, and procrastinate. This doesn't plague only salon owners, it's a problem for all people in service businesses. So much of a problem, in fact, that many have found a solution: Sending out reminders.

The dealership where you bought your car may send you a reminder saying that their records indicate your car is ready for an oil change or some other such service. Dentists send out reminders all the time saying that you haven't been in for a check up since such-and-such date, and you're overdue. They make it sound as though they're doing you a favor by calling this matter to your attention. Doctors get in the act by sending out reminders in the fall suggesting that patients come in for their flu shots. You, too, should jump on the reminder bandwagon.

The two highest volume services in salons right now are cutting and coloring, both of which should be repeated periodically. Perming surely should be repeated every several months. Even conditioning, which doesn't necessarily have to be done at specific intervals, should really be done to everybody at certain times of the year—at the end of the summer, for example, when hair has been subjected to the usual summer abuses. Any or all of these services can use reminders, and the reminders can be simple post cards. They don't cost very much to mail, they don't cost very much to print. Here are some guideposts to keep in mind as you do your thinking, planning, and evaluation as to whether or not to go with this kind of promotion.

1 You must—must!—keep accurate records of what services you perform on which clients. If you don't know who came in when and what they came in for, you can't possibly remind them to come in for the same service again at an appropriate interval.

2 You can have postcards printed in a typeface or have them handwritten and then duplicated by your printer. If you have a computer and have the appropriate program, you can have the cards printed and personalized right in the salon.

3 Your copy can read something like:

Dear Mrs. Jones,

We had the pleasure of cutting your hair several weeks ago on June 12th. Right about now it should be just about ready to be recut and reshaped. Won't you please call for an appointment? We'd be delighted to serve you.

Shear Artistry

4 Of course, you can change that copy and format to suit you and the personality of your salon. You can have the cards personally signed by specific stylists. Make the copy chattier, less formal. You must use your own type of communication and your own relationships with your clientele in drafting the copy.

5 Would you like to sweeten the reminder with an incentive for them to act now? Offer them a free product or an in-salon conditioning treatment when they bring the card in. The number of laggards you flush out, the number of appointments the cards will generate, will more than offset the cost of your incentives.

6 Don't send your reminder cards out monthly. That might generate too many appointments, and you'll have a clogged schedule. Send them out weekly so that the appointments they generate will be spread out and not create a logjam.

7 If the client has several different renewable services all on one day, the services probably won't all repeat at the exact same time. So she'll get a reminder card for each individual service.

DON'T BE SHY ABOUT SENDING REMINDER CARDS. YOUR CLIENTS WILL ACTUALLY APPRECIATE THEM.

Don't be shy about sending reminder cards. Your clients won't object to them; they'll actually appreciate them. They'll know you're thinking of them and keeping track of their needs.

This promotion is ongoing, it never stops. It takes record keeping, it takes discipline, it takes organization. The rewards for all this? Greater client retention, appreciation, awareness that you are attentive to their needs and more traffic. Not bad rewards, wouldn't you say?

Wall of Achievement

PREPARATION TIME

RESPECT BEGETS
LOYALTY, AND LOYALTY
BEGETS DOLLARS IN THE
CASH REGISTER.

Most clients don't really know how skilled you and your staff are, how endlessly you improve your craft by classes, clinics, and seminars. Clients have more faith, confidence, and admiration for people who perform personal services and are constantly adding to their knowledge. This applies whether the service person is an auto mechanic who's just completed a factory training class at General Motors or a surgeon who has just attended a conference on a new surgical procedure.

But we don't blow our horns often enough in our industry. We attend manufacturers' classes on every aspect of the salon industry. We take special instruction with renowned stylists. Certainly we return with greater knowledge with which to serve our clients, but they don't really know about it. And if the new knowledge is in a particular service that they're not getting, you can't even demonstrate your new knowledge to them. Nonetheless, if they knew that you had this new knowledge, they would respect you for it. And respect begets loyalty, and loyalty begets dollars in the cash register.

We've got to get across to every client who goes through the salon the fact that within the four walls of this salon there exists an enormous amount of knowledge. How to make this point is not particularly difficult. We're going to set up a Wall of Achievement. Here are some tips on how to do it.

1 Make sure that every person who works in your salon and attends any type of educational function whatsoever gets some sort of evidence of their attendance. Many courses and classes automatically issue diplomas or certificates, but many more just give you the education and that's that. No, we are not going to be satisfied merely with the new knowledge we've received. We want some sort of documentation. It's not hard. Ask whoever is in charge of the class to simply write a letter acknowledging the individual's attendance and perhaps putting in a flowery phrase or two like, "This was an advanced class, and I admire your professionalism in seeking always to upgrade your knowledge in this aspect of your craft." Leave it to the writers. They'll always come up with something special.

2 Every letter, every diploma, every certificate should be framed. Generally speaking, it's good to frame them all identically so that your credentials wall doesn't look like a hodgepodge. A simple black frame will do for each document. It will draw attention to the document rather than the frame.

3 For these framed licenses, letters, certificates, diplomas, or other evidences of achievement, don't choose a wall somewhere in the back where few will see it. No, choose a location that every client in the salon can't miss.

4 Have a sign made up at the top of the wall, above all the framed credentials, that says:

WALL OF ACHIEVEMENT

WE AT THE NEW IMAGE SALON CONSIDER IT OUR PROFESSIONAL OBLIGATION TO CONSTANTLY, CONTINUALLY, ENDLESSLY INCREASE OUR CREATIVE AND TECHNICAL AND ARTISTIC ABILITIES, TO BETTER SERVE YOU. THUS, OUR CLIENTS MAY BE ASSURED THAT EACH OF OUR COSMETOLOGISTS IS AT THE CUTTING EDGE OF STATE-OF-THE-ART KNOWLEDGE.

5 The Wall of Achievement would make a fantastic window display at least one a year, maybe twice. Obviously you can't move an entire wall, so instead you can mount all the framed documents on a sheet of painted plywood. Depending on how many documents you have, you can get sheets of plywood in many sizes, up to 4′ × 8′. In fact, for most of the year that entire sheet of plywood, together with the framed documents, can itself be mounted on a wall and will constitute your wall of Achievement. When you want to move the "wall," unscrew the sheet of plywood and move the whole shebang into your window.

AS THE SAYING GOES, "WHEN YOU GOT IT, FLAUNT IT!"

6 The display of everyone's achievements will actually motivate your staff to get more diplomas, more certificates, more letters. To encourage them to upgrade their knowledge still further, you might give some sort of special award, gift, or bonus to the individual who accumulates the greatest number of achievement documents in a twelve-month period.

As the saying goes, "When you got it, flaunt it!"

Promo 88

"Guaranteed Satisfaction" Beauty Experience

PREPARATION TIME

What most clients and potential clients want out of their salon visit is a satisfactory experience. If they're unhappy, even in a small way, it won't matter that the price may have been low. If your prices are in the upper range, it makes things that much worse. But even if they're in the lower range, it doesn't excuse unhappiness. A lot of potential clients out there aren't too thrilled with their current salon experiences, but they aren't necessarily so unhappy that they actively want to switch. They feel that the next place may not be any better. You've got to get these folks and convince them that their salon experience *will* be better and that you absolutely, positively, unequivocally *guarantee* it!

We don't know who these potential clients are or where they are. We just know they're out there. That being the case, you've got to reach them by whatever means your budget can afford.

1 Do you have an advertising budget with enough in it for an ad campaign? Then newspaper advertising would be your best choice. Speak to the advertising department of the newspaper. Find out what day of the week is best for advertising to women. Plan on no less than once a week for at least a month.

2 Can you afford to advertise but with a less generous sum? Postcards are always effective. You'll have to buy a mailing list of the zip code area you want to reach, and you'll have to pay for the printing, addressing, and postage.

3 Perhaps a little more economical would be to get your message across in the Yellow Pages. Rates vary greatly from one community to the next. You'll have to check them out. If you go this route, your "guaranteed satisfaction" message will be the same, and it will be out there for a whole year.

4 Printed flyers are the most economical way to go. You can have one of your staff handing them out near supermarkets, just on the street in highly trafficked areas, placed under windshield wipers in parking lots, or slipped under the doors of apartment houses. You get the idea. You know your locality. Wherever there are people is where your flyers should be distributed.

Getting the message out by one method of distribution or another is, of course, vital. More vital is the message itself. We want to get the potential client's attention, and we want to give her a message she hasn't seen before. Make the message suitable to your salon's personality and your potential clientele. But however you word it, you should keep these important ingredients:

MAKE A STRONG, CLEAR STATEMENT OF YOUR PROMISE, YOUR GUARANTEE.

1 Have it look like a guarantee *document* so the client gets the idea right away.

2 Have a representative of beauty, either by the reproduction of a photograph or a line drawing. We want to instantly let the client know that this guarantee has nothing to do with appliances. We are talking beauty here and a photo or drawing will click immediately.

3 Use a strong headline like GUARANTEED BEAUTY. The object is for a woman to see it and think, "What's this all about? Let me read further." Hopefully Guaranteed Beauty will do the trick. If you can think of a better hook, by all means use it.

Make a strong, clear statement of your promise, your guarantee, such as:

4 At Master Design Salon we don't want our clients to be satisfied or even very satisfied. Our aim is TOTAL satisfaction! Our cosmetologists are experts in every facet of beauty and appearance. Whether it's a simple manicure or a complete makeover, our **guarantee** is that you *will* be totally satisfied. If your satisfaction is less than total, we will either redo the service until it is absolutely "right" or there will be no charge. This is our pledge, our **guarantee**, to you.

Call for an appointment today. Experience for yourself what it feels like to be totally satisfied with your salon experience.

Master Design, 1234 Elm Street, Lakeview, MI, Tel. 987-6543

NOTES

That guarantee places an enormous responsibility on you and your staff. Do you have the confidence to live up to it? If so, go for it. If you don't have this confidence, it's a signal to trade up the capabilities of your salon.

Don't worry about the occasional crank who may come along and who may simply never be satisfied. Clients like this will always be in the minority, and under the worst of conditions you will have performed some services you received no revenue for. Counterbalancing that will be the many who will like the idea that your salon is confident enough in its abilities to offer this extraordinary guarantee. The pluses will outweigh the minuses by far.

Put Out Your
Own Newsletter

"Put out my own newsletter? Impossible! What do I know about putting out a newsletter?" If that's your reaction, relax. Don't turn the page and go on to the next promotion. Linger a bit and let's explore.

Keep in mind how important communication is. You've got a certain number of people working in your salon. You yourself may be behind a chair, and you've got to run full-speed ahead just to keep the ship afloat and headed in the right direction. In all this activity, isn't it possible (even probable) that communication with clients may fall through the cracks? And is there anything more important then an ongoing, productive, and constructive line of communication with these clients? You want a certain dialogue flowing back and forth between your clientele, your salon, and yourself. A newsletter can be the bedrock that all this communication is founded on. Don't just reject the idea. Think about it.

It's not as hard as you may think. In fact, once you get into it, you'll find it easy. Do you have a gift for communicating via the written word? We're not talking literature here. We're not talking deathless prose. We're talking about the ability to write a folksy, newsy letter to a friend. If you can do that, you can write a newsletter. If you can't, or if you're too busy, how about one of your employees? Surely the talent exists right there in the salon. Or perhaps you have a friend or relative who actually enjoys writing. This will be their opportunity.

The next question that arises is, "What is there to write about?" Here's a quick dozen areas that will always give you more than enough material.

YOU WANT A CERTAIN DIALOGUE FLOWING BACK AND FORTH BETWEEN YOUR CLIENTELE, YOUR SALON, AND YOURSELF. A NEWSLETTER CAN BE THE BEDROCK THAT ALL THIS COMMUNICATION IS FOUNDED ON.

1. News of recently added service.
2. Introduction of new retail lines or products.
3. Personal news of your staff that might interest your clients.
4. Announcements of competitions entered and, better yet, won.
5. Any write-ups or publicity your salon has received.
6. How-tos, makeup tips, fashion forecasts, home care, style reports.
7. Coupons for retail and/or specials or discounts.
8. A calendar of your salon promotions, demonstrations, events.
9. Photos of clients with their new cuts.

10. Congrats to clients who've had birthdays, weddings, newborns, and the like.
11. Reports of visits to trade shows and what you learned.
12. Reports of seminars, clinics, classes your staff has attended and what they learned.

You don't have to be overly ambitious. A two-page newsletter (one sheet front and back) will do—and it's cheap. Never, never go beyond four pages. That's too much. The client probably won't read it—and it's expensive.

You don't need fancy, heavy paper. Standard $8\frac{1}{2} \times 11$ bond will do the trick. Printing on colored paper can be somewhat more effective and hardly more expensive than plain white.

Once you've gotten the information written, now comes the "hard" part. It wasn't too long ago that you'd have had to go to a printer to set it all in type. That was an expensive process. Now it's practically free. Do you have a computer with a word processing program or have access to one? If you aren't computer literate (as I am not), don't despair. You can probably find someone, maybe even one of your kids, to do it for minimal compensation. If all else fails, go to your local high school. It might be willing to lay out your newsletter as a class exercise.

As to making copies, virtually every town and hamlet in America has a Quick Print, Kinko's, or local office supplies store that will do the copy job for you, often while you wait.

How many should you send out? Good question. Certainly every current client should get your newsletter. Positively every former client, too. Then ask these very people (you can do it right in the newsletter) to submit names of their friends who may be interested in receiving the kind of information you're putting forth. You can, of course, buy mailing lists, but at the beginning it might be best to first put out two or three newsletters so that you get the rhythm and the style before you go to the expense of buying lists.

Finally, how often should you publish? Very rarely do salon newsletters go out monthly. By and large, every other month will prove very effective. If that's not comfortable, do it quarterly as each of the seasons approaches. If it's less than quarterly, you start to lose the continuity. If you can only manage to do it twice a year, the effectiveness will be diminished. Shoot for four to six times a year.

You're going to be very pleasantly surprised. If your newsletter contains coupons, clients will cut them out and bring them in. When you comment on weddings, graduations, and births, they'll appreciate it. When you publish a photo or drawing of a cut or style, some will tell you, "That's just what I want." When all this happens, you'll be communicating—clients with you, you with them—and that is, after all, the object of the whole exercise, isn't it?

PUBLISHING A NEWSLETTER EVERY OTHER MONTH WILL PROVE VERY EFFECTIVE.

Declare
"Hair Health Month"

It is the rare woman, young or old, who is satisfied with the condition of her hair. It's dry or it's stringy or she's got frizzies or static electricity. Maybe her hair won't hold a style or color. She may have dandruff or, indeed, any one of dozens of different problems. If you had a room full of one hundred women and asked how many were completely satisfied with the health and condition of their hair, not too many hands would be raised. This presents a terrific opportunity. You can declare "Hair Health Month" (or "Hair Health Week" or "Mondays are Hair Health Days" or whatever). How do you do it? Here are some guides.

PREPARATION TIME

1   Tell people about it by sending postcards to a mailing list or taking a series of small ads in your local newspaper, or simply by putting a big sign in your window.

2   During the Hair Health period you and/or designated stylists will give free hair and scalp examinations and consultations as a public service. The consultations should be absolutely free, not obligate the "patients," and not require appointments. If people come in when you're jammed to the gills, you can courteously explain that everyone is totally booked at the moment but to come back at such-and-such time, and you'll be able to devote a decent amount of time to the examination of their hair and scalp.

3   Everyone who comes in for the free examination and consultation should, of course, give you their name and address, and during the course of the consultation you'll learn lots more about them. Don't rush the consultee, and surely don't pressure her. Be totally professional, and ask a lot of questions. When you give your conclusions and evaluations, don't automatically shove a product in her face. Tell her what her problems are, tell her what brought about these problems, tell her what the solutions are, be they products or services.

PEOPLE'S

DISSATISFACTION

WITH THEIR HAIR

PRESENTS A TERRIFIC

OPPORTUNITY.

4 Be assured that when you tell the woman what types of shampoos she should use, she will ask for you recommendations as to brand. She will surely need some kind of conditioning and conditioners. Again, she'll ask what you suggest. Don't be greedy. Don't load her up with products she doesn't need. Do prescribe products and procedures you honestly feel she does need.

5 When the woman buys any of your product, as she inevitably will, assure her that you absolutely guarantee the products if she follows your advice and usage. If the products and procedures don't solve the problems she came in to learn about and discuss, be certain to tell her she will get a complete refund.

6 Be certain to tell any of your stylists who participate in this program to keep the selling "soft." The whole procedure will be much more effective if the people who come in for consultations get a feeling of friendliness, professionalism, technical know-how, and sincere desire to help. That way, even if a woman doesn't buy any products, she'll be impressed enough to recommend friends to you.

You can be certain that if consultations are handled properly, people will generally walk out with at least one and probably several of the products that come up during the consultation. In many cases they'll book an appointment. In any event you'll have names, addresses, and other particulars for future promotional mailings. It's all pluses and no minuses.

When the promotion is over, your salon will be identified with hair therapy and good hair condition, and that will surely help bring in business for the rest of the year—until you do the promotion all over again next year.

Tell Your Clients You're Always Learning

PREPARATION TIME

If you own a salon where you, your stylists, colorists, and nail artists make it a practice to attend educational events on a fairly frequent and ongoing basis, this promotion is for you. If your staff is lethargic and doesn't keep going and keep learning, sorry, you'll have to pass this one by.

Take it as an article of faith that your clients want you to keep learning and want you to keep up with the latest trends and technologies in beauty. Be assured, *they* keep up. They read the womens' fashion magazines and the Sunday supplements, and they watch all sorts of beauty presentations on cable TV. If you don't keep up with *them*, you're in deep trouble. But the point is not simply to keep up with the level of knowledge of your clientele but to get way out there in front so that by the time they read about it, you've been talking about it or doing it for months.

One of the joys of our industry is that there's an endless stream of classes, clinics, seminars, workshops, and shows available to all cosmetologists in virtually all parts of the country. In addition, we have great trade publications in our country and a seemingly infinite number of publications available from other countries. If you want to learn, there are many, *many* opportunities for you and your staff to do so.

As you, and the people working for you, learn more and more, and get better and better at what you all do, your clients will, of course, be delighted with the increasingly better results. You can get much more "bang for the buck," much more mileage, respect, and admiration, if you all don't just quietly improve your skills but if you *promote*. One of the simplest, most effective, and least expensive ways to promote your educational activities is by postcard.

Your basic mailing list should be everyone who has come into your salon in the last two or three years. At the beginning it will be mostly your existing clients whom you want to impress. They're the ones who are already loyal, and when they start getting all of this information about the ongoing improvement of your staff, it will seep into their conversations when they talk to friends. And it will sink deeper roots into your salon. After two or three mailings to your existing clients, you can start going beyond. Get additional mailings from list houses, mens' clubs, womens' clubs, and names your clients

ONE OF THE SIMPLEST, MOST EFFECTIVE, AND LEAST EXPENSIVE WAYS TO PROMOTE YOUR EDUCATIONAL ACTIVITIES IS BY POSTCARD.

suggest to you. What to say? Here's a suggestion, but remember you can surely choose your own wording.

> We at Gloria's Total Image Salon are constantly training, constantly improving our skills. Various of our staff attend classes, clinics, seminars, shows, and workshops on a continuing basis. In the last two months here are some of the educational events some of us have attended . . .
>
> Edy—Clairol Color Classes, March 21, March 28, April 4
> Dot—Same as Edy
> Debbie—Haircutting Class with Michael Forsythe of Beverly Hills, April 12
> Terry—Same as Debbie
> Ida—Nail Art Seminar and Workshop, April 4, April 11
>
> We all try to stay at the leading edge of product technology, styling techniques, and fashion. Come see for yourself.
>
> Gloria's Total Image Salon, 987 North Avenue, Southwick, KN, Tel: 456-7890

Ideally it would be nice to mail these cards out every month as a reminder of the talents in your salon. If you don't want to go for that expense monthly, or if you don't have that many things to report in any given month, do it bimonthly, quarterly, or even semiannually, depending on your budget and how many things you want to crow about to your clientele.

If you want to make it fancier, you can have photos taken of everyone in the salon and print little miniatures of the appropriate staff who participated in educational events since the last mailing. But that's really not necessary. Postcards will stand on their own with a simple, straightforward message.

Unlike newspapers—which your clients may not buy or may buy and not read on any given day or may just skim through—when a client sees your postcard, she'll read it. It's not junk mail. It's an out-of-the-ordinary communication. It will only take her a few seconds to go through your message, but in those few seconds an impression will be made of people she's familiar with bettering themselves for her benefit. Chances are she'll remark about it on the next visit.

In a month, or two, or three, or whatever, she'll get another mailing that will reinforce this respect. Then, after an interval, she'll get yet another mailing. No one can help being impressed. And your client will be. And she'll tell her friends, and she'll compliment you, and she'll have more and more services performed in the salon . . . and everybody will be happy.

Signs on the Ceiling Could Boost Your Tuesdays

An old song used to lament that "Saturday night is the loneliest night of the week." In most salons we can paraphrase that to "Tuesday is the loneliest day of the week." What to do? Wouldn't it be worthwhile to fill those empty chairs by offering a discount on services on Tuesdays? Of course. Here's a way to do it with a bit of creativity.

PREPARATION TIME

1 Have signs made up to put **on the ceiling** over each shampoo bowl. The signs should read:

> YOU COULD'VE SAVED 20 PERCENT ON THE SERVICES YOU'RE HAVING BY BOOKING ON TUESDAY!

DISCOUNT OFFER

2 Just to make sure the sign is noticed and talked about, dangle dollar bills from the signs.

Will the signs be noticed? Of course. Will clients find them amusing? Sure. Will they talk about it with their stylists? Positively.

Of course, you could post a sign telling of the promotion in your reception area or in your window. But that wouldn't bring smiles or cause the same amount of conversation. It's the ceiling bit that will make it successful.

WHEN CHAIRS ARE EMPTY, YOU'RE LOSING MONEY. WHEN CHAIRS ARE OCCUPIED BUT WITH SERVICES AT A DISCOUNT, YOU'RE MAKING MONEY.

3 The full promotion is that the clients should be informed that the discount (10 percent, 20 percent, or whatever) applies to every service in the salon. This will encourage them to go for more services, thus actually increasing the average client ticket rather than decreasing it. It would even be good to extend the same discount (or perhaps a somewhat lesser one) to all retail merchandise bought on Tuesdays.

Is it worth it to have a busier Tuesday book even though the average profit per client may be somewhat diminished? No doubt about it! When chairs are empty, you're losing money. When chairs are occupied but with services at a discount, you're making money. Where's the comparison?

NOTES

If you do this promotion, it will take just about five to ten minutes of your time after closing time on Tuesday to put up the signs. Leave them up from Wednesday through Saturday; then take them down last thing before you leave on Saturday night.

Clients will catch on very quickly—in fact, immediately—that the smart thing to do is book on Tuesdays. With many people, booking toward the end of the week is simply a habit, not a necessity. In the old wash 'n set days, they wanted to come in at the end of the week because the style had to be put in place, glued with spray, and last until the next appointment. Not anymore. It truly doesn't make too much difference to the average client whether she gets her hair cut on Friday or on Tuesday. How about color highlights? Tuesday, Wednesday, Thursday, Friday, Saturday—what's the difference?

The signs on the ceiling offering the discounts will serve as behavior modification, and it won't be too many weeks before Tuesdays will become just as busy as any of the other days of the week. At that time you may choose to discontinue this promotion. If you do, remember that the device of the ceiling signs is still potent. These signs will be seen by every single client. So you can send any message you'd like. Once clients are used to seeing these signs, they'll look for them.

When you don't have anything special to say, it will always be appropriate to convey the message "We're glad you're here."

Keep Your Doors Open the Hours When Your Customers Want to Come In

PREPARATION TIME

Just about all of your clients fall into the 18 to 64 age group. Studies indicate that better than half of all women in this group are currently in the labor force. They're working women. They're not ladies of leisure. They're not retired. When do they work, what are their hours? Chances are they're mostly in or around the 9 to 5 time frame. If your salon hours are approximately 9 to 5, that means you're closed when these women go to work in the morning and closed when they come home at night. What's the solution for these working gals?

1) They decide to handle all their hair and beauty needs at home.

2) They book their appointments on Saturday—the day you're busiest and don't need more appointments.

Neither of these "solutions" helps your business. Let's try some other solutions.

1 You're in a service business and your number one objective has to be to best serve your clients. You've got to take a long, hard look at your hours. You may want to open earlier in the morning and stay open later at night. If you're in a downtown area, advertising or publicizing early-bird hours will be enthusiastically welcomed. If the client can get the service she wants before starting her day's work, she'll be a happy camper and will absolutely be locked in to you because there won't be too many other salons she'll be able to go to before 9 A.M. Similarly, however, if you're not in a downtown area, there may still be a significant number of clients who would like to come in for their salon services before getting into the car or carpool and driving to work.

2 Then there are the night hours. Many's the woman who'd be willing to finish her day's work and plop into a salon to have her touch-up, her cut, or a facial treatment. They know that if they take care of their beauty services during the week, they won't have to sacrifice part of a Saturday to have them done. That is a huge benefit for these women.

YOU'RE IN A SERVICE BUSINESS AND YOUR NUMBER ONE OBJECTIVE HAS TO BE TO BEST SERVE YOUR CLIENTS.

3 Finally there's the matter of Sundays. There are all kinds of reasons why salon owners and stylists simply don't want to work on Sunday, and that is certainly understandable. But many salons have experimented with Sunday hours and have been successful with them.

Very obviously, expanding your hours so that you open earlier, keep open later, and maybe open on Sundays does *not* mean that either you or any of your staff should work twelve hours a day, six or seven days a week. First you'll have to determine whether you should open earlier *and* stay open later *and* open on Sundays. Take two to three months to poll your clients. Discuss it with them. Discuss it with your employees. You may want to work out a combination arrangement whereby you open early perhaps three days a week, and stay open late perhaps two days a week. There's no way to make one set of rules for every salon. It all depends on a host of variables and your clients' opinions and preferences hold the key to how successful your changes will be.

As for staff, you'll have to do some very specific recruiting. Some will actually prefer coming in early and leaving early. Some would rather come in later and leave later. And believe it or not, there will be some who would rather work on Sundays and have an extra day in the middle of the week off. When you have satisfied yourself that you know what you think will be a successful expansion of hours, you don't have to consider it written in stone. Try it for maybe three months. If it builds during that time, keep the changes. If it doesn't, make adjustments.

WHEN YOU FIND THE

RIGHT COMBINATION OF

ANSWERS CONCERNING

HOURS, THE BUSINESS

WILL BE THERE.

If you do change your hours, you can't be too quiet or subtle about it. Go through this book and pick out some promotional ideas that will help get the word out not only to your existing clients but to potential new clients, as well. If you're the only one in your area with these expanded hours, it may actually be newsworthy. Try to contact the beauty editor of your neighborhood newspaper. Invite her to come in herself for a free visit at 7:30 in the morning or perhaps 7:30 at night.

Signs in the windows, postcards, flyers, discounts, promotions, any or all of these devices can and should be used. Just know that when you're exploring this whole area, you're searching for how you may better serve your clientele. When you find the right combination of answers concerning hours, the business will be there, and you'll ask yourself, "Why didn't we think of this before?"

Nothing Like a Straight, Simple Story

Advertising scares a lot of people. So does promotion and public relations. They think you need extraordinary talent and training, and to a great degree they're right. But when we're talking about a local salon, we don't need the background needed to plan a national campaign for Coca-Cola. OK, you just opened a small one, two, or three station salon and can't see budgeting too significant an amount announcing your arrival in the town or neighborhood. But you also don't want to open and simply hang out and wait around to be discovered. What to do? You just need to get the message out to appropriate people in the local trading area. This can be relatively simple.

PREPARATION TIME

PRINTED MATERIAL

1 Have a flyer printed that contains the message you want to get across. (We'll get to the message in a moment). The flyer should be printed on standard 8½ × 11 colored paper. Or it can be laid out to fit 8½ × 5½. In this way you can have the message printed twice on the standard 8½ × 11 paper, and cut right across the middle. That cuts your printing costs in half.

2 If it's appropriate and not against any local ordinances, you can stand on a street corner or in a busy shopping center, and distribute the flyers to pedestrians.

3 Speak to whoever delivers the local newspapers in the neighborhood. Very often they'll be willing to distribute merchants' advertising right along with the papers.

4 Look up "Mailing Lists" in the Yellow Pages. You'd be amazed that some list houses may have the exact consumers you want to reach. If you send your flyers through the mail, it would be less expensive to have your message printed on postcards. Postage on cards is currently 20¢, so one hundred postcards would be $20; one thousand cards would be $200. Not bad at all.

5 You simply want to let people know that you're there. What could be more simple than just saying:

HI!

I'm your new
hairstylist
in the neighborhood!

RONNIE JONES

at

RONNIE'S HAIRSTYLING

123 North Street
Dunkirk, NY
987-6543

PRECISION CUTTING, PERMING,
COLORING, CONDITIONING

PEOPLE WILL READ

A SIMPLE MESSAGE

THAT CONTAINS ONLY

A FEW WORDS. AND

PEOPLE WILL RESPOND

IF THOSE FEW WORDS

HIT THE SPOT.

Want to use your photo? Go ahead. Want to give them an incentive like "Bring in this flyer for a 10 percent discount on all services and products?" By all means.

At any given time a certain number of beauty salon clients in every locality are unhappy with their salon. If they're severely unhappy, they'll start asking around for recommendations from their friends. If they're just ordinarily unhappy, they may go plodding along because they don't have an immediately viable alternative. When one of these ladies gets one of your flyers, she'll think, "How'd they know I was unhappy? I think I'll give them a call right now!" Bingo!

People *will* read a simple message that contains only a few words. And people *will* respond if those few words hit the spot. The cost is absolutely minimal, and you won't have to simply open your small salon and wait.

Consider Mondays

PREPARATION TIME

A lot of habits and policies are deeply ingrained in the salon business. Things like a 50 percent commission for hairstylists. That's still around, and it's still the standard in many salons. But many others have employed newer, more innovative compensation plans. Employee benefits? No, salons couldn't afford them and simply don't make them available to a great percentage of employees. Yet many salons have crafted all sorts of ways in which they have managed to offer at least some sort of benefit package. And then there's the policy of being closed on Monday. After all, the five day, forty-hour week is standard in American industry. Why shouldn't that apply to salons?

The answer is that we are living in different economic times. Many people want or need to work more than standard eight-hour days to earn additional income. Many take a second job on the weekend for the same reason. Maybe you don't remember that *all* stores used to be closed on Sundays, which is certainly not so any longer. And yes, even though the vast majority of salons don't open on Monday, there is an ever increasing number that do, and always for the same reason: to maximize income.

Salons we're always closed on Mondays to give owner and employees two consecutive days off. They can still get two consecutive days off, but do those two days have to be Sunday and Monday? Could they be two other days? And aren't there some employees who, for personal reasons, wouldn't necessarily insist on two consecutive days off? People live complex lives nowadays. Flexible hours, flexible times, flexible days are concepts whose times have come.

FLEXIBLE HOURS, FLEXIBLE TIMES, FLEXIBLE DAYS ARE CONCEPTS WHOSE TIMES HAVE COME.

There *are* stylists who would be willing to work on Mondays, either full days or at least half days. It would simply take a little work, a little probing on your part to find them, perhaps not only among your current staff but also people looking for employment.

The difficulty in making this project work isn't getting employees. You'll get them. It's getting clients to come in on Mondays. We have spent so many decades training generations of clients that salons were closed on Mondays that it may take a while to make your community fully aware that you're open on Monday. There are a number of ways you can do it.

NOTES

1. Put up a big sign in your window saying:

> **For the convenience of our clients, we are now**
> OPEN ON MONDAYS

2. Put up smaller signs in the reception area and at each station saying:

> **For your convenience,**
> **we are now open on Mondays.**

3. Take small ads in local publications saying:

> A SALON APPOINTMENT IS A WONDERFUL WAY TO START THE WEEK.
> **Beauty, Inc. is now open on Mondays.**

4. If you have an ad in the Yellow Pages, make sure it emphasizes that you are open on Mondays.

5. If your neighborhood lends itself to it, you can pass out a few hundred flyers announcing your Monday policy. Pass them out wherever you aren't prohibited from doing so.

6. Have whoever answers the phone in your salon say this greeting to every caller: "New Image Salon. We are now open on Mondays. May I help you?" Do that for a month or two—or three. The message *will* sink in; you *will* start to cultivate a Monday clientele.

7. At the start, and for as long as you have to, discount Monday services heavily, or give away a free retail product with each appointment.

8. Try to convert as many of your existing clients to Monday appointments. The more end-of-the-week appointments you can switch to Mondays, the more openings you'll have to accommodate clients who can only come in on Fridays and Saturdays.

Yes, it may take a little while to build up the Monday business, but it will all be worth it. When your salon has six days in which to accumulate its gross income instead of five days, you have the possibility of dramatically increasing your take. YOUR BIGGEST OBSTACLE IS GOING TO BE HABIT—HABIT ON YOUR PART, HABIT ON YOUR EMPLOYEE'S PART, HABIT ON YOUR CLIENT'S PART. But we all know that habits can be changed, and this habit certainly is one of them.

Now, dare we say it, keep in mind that everything noted above with regard to Mondays can also apply to Sundays.

MISCELLANEOUS

Promo 96

Make Monday Night Makeover Night

Will the American consumer ever tire of makeover photos? The answer is no. And the proof lies in all the womens' fashion and service magazines. Scarcely a month goes by without one or more of these magazines doing a feature article on makeovers. People just love to see them. When they look at them, they often wish that they could have a competent, professional makeover. People write to magazines all the time volunteering themselves as subjects for future makeover articles. Be assured that many of your clients, many of those women sitting in your chairs in your salon, have a curiosity about what they would look like if they were "made over." You can satisfy this curiosity, build business, and make an unproductive time—Monday night—into a profit center.

1. You must be certain that the talent exists in your salon to really do competent analyses and execute competent makeovers. Let's face it, not everyone can do beautiful makeovers. Some haircutters only have a repertoire of a few different cuts. Many cosmetologists don't know all the principles of makeup, color coordination, shadowing, and so on. So the first thing you have to do is be convinced yourself that the talent exists to do A-to-Z makeovers.

THE EMPHASIS SHOULD
BE ON MAKEOVERS
THAT THE CLIENTS CAN
CONTINUE THEMSELVES.

2. This is a new activity, so you can start it slowly and expand it as you learn more about the whole procedure. The emphasis should be on makeovers that the clients can continue themselves. Therefore, it's not merely a matter of executing the makeovers, it's a matter of executing them and teaching the clients how to continue them.

3. A complete makeover can take several hours just to do the execution part, not including the instruction part. Therefore, clients who are interested in the makeover service should be signed up for three sessions, each session two hours long. That's enough to give them their money's worth but not too much to make a serious dent in their own schedule and availability.

4 This promotion is not one to advertise in the newspapers. Remember, you want to start off slowly. You can start with a small sign in the salon that says:

MONDAY NIGHT IS MAKEOVER NIGHT . . . WE CAN ACCEPT A LIMITED NUMBER OF CLIENTS FOR MONDAY EVENING MAKEOVER SESSIONS, TO ANALYZE ALL ASPECTS OF YOUR BEAUTY PRESENTATION, FACE, HAIR, NAILS, SKIN, MAKEUP AND THEN TO INSTRUCT YOU IN THE MAINTENANCE OF YOUR NEW LOOK. SESSIONS RUN FROM 7 TO 9 P.M. TOTAL COST FOR THE THREE SESSIONS IN $75. YOUR SATISFACTION IS GUARANTEED.

5 Each and every member of your staff must be thoroughly briefed as to what will be happening on makeover night. Not all will participate, but all will benefit because of the goodwill of the clients and the additional services they'll be exposed to.

6 Once "Monday Is Makeover Night" gets rolling with existing clientele, you can put a sign in your window that says something like:

MONDAY IS MAKEOVER NIGHT . . . INQUIRE INSIDE

You'll get nibbles, you'll get questions, you'll get bookings. Remember, once clients are booked for three nights, they're yours.

7 Ask everyone who signs up for the program to bring their own makeup, their own styling tools, their own shampoos, conditioners, gels, and sprays. If you're going to teach them what products to use for their new look and how to use them, you have to know what they're working with at home. Much of the makeup will be unusable in their new look, thus giving you the opportunity to sell them the new products they'll need. Same goes for their hairstyles. The potential for substantial retail sales from each person who signs up is enormous.

> THE POTENTIAL FOR SUBSTANTIAL RETAIL SALES FROM EACH PERSON WHO SIGNS UP IS ENORMOUS.

The details of this kind of program are not written in stone. You can charge more than I have suggested or less. You can have one long makeover session, if you clients will sit still for it, rather than three two-hour sessions. You can choose a night other than Monday. However you customize and craft your makeover nights, you'll find that you'll get several guaranteed, locked-in advantages.

- Because of the great individualized attention and the total focus being on the client, these clients will become incredibly loyal.

YOU'LL ALL GET TO

USE PROFESSIONAL

SKILLS THAT YOU OFTEN

DON'T HAVE TIME TO

DEMONSTRATE DURING

REGULAR SALON HOURS.

- They'll automatically buy whatever product, shades of product, formulations of product you mutually agree on to be part of their made-over look.

- In many cases noncolor clients will opt for color services. Same thing with perms. This is all new business.

- When clients are done, they'll scarcely be able to contain themselves. They'll want to show off their new look and tell their friends. Results? More new business, more new clients.

You and your stylists will also enjoy these evenings. They're much more relaxed than the daytime schedules, and you'll all get to use professional skills that you often don't have time to demonstrate during regular salon hours.

Take a Tip from the Movies

MISCELLANEOUS

The people who market movies found a terrific gimmick. Instead of taxing their advertising and promotional people to come up with great copy describing new films, they show the films first to critics, then excerpt words or phrases from the critics' reviews and use those words and phrases as advertising copy. Very clever: "Don't take our word that this is the greatest film in the history of cinema. Look at what these guys say." Read the quotes carefully, and you'll find they often come from obscure critics in distant cities. But who cares? It's the big words—"Electrifying!" "Stupendous!" "Oscar-worthy performance"—that works. Even if you don't know who the critic is, you figure it's someone who's supposed to know what they're doing, so maybe you'll go see the film.

The focus of this book is not to spend big money on full-page ads in newspapers. Our mission is to get the job done on shoestring budgets. Toward this end, we can use the principle the movies use: testimonials. Let's see how we can use this principle to bring more bodies into your salon.

1 During the course of any day and surely in the course of a week there are clients who are particularly pleased with their stylist, colorist, manicurist, esthetician and the service she/he performed. They're vocal about it. They want you to know.

2 When this happens spontaneously, ask the client if she would do a great favor for you. Would she be kind enough to jot down her reactions and sign it? The note can be a few sentences long or one comprehensive sentence. Something like "My hair has never been in such beautiful condition as it's been since Judy is taking care of it." Wouldn't that be sensational? A few words like "Best haircut I've had in years" would be equally great. "Glorious color" is just a two-word description, but it tells the whole story eloquently.

UTILIZE THE PRINCIPLE OF MOVIE ADVERTISING: TESTIMONIALS.

3 Try to get the client to write the note right there on the spot. If she promises to do it when she gets home, chances are she won't. Other priorities will take precedence the minute she gets through the door. So give her an index card and a pen and ask her to do it then and there. Most times she'll cooperate.

4 Now tell her that it's possible you may want to use her words in some advertising and promotion, and if she agrees, the next time she has the service she just raved about will be with your compliments. If she says yes, as she most certainly will do, ask her to attach a note giving you permission to use her words. (You may want to ask your attorney if certain phraseology should be used here.)

5 When you're looking to build a specific stylist, wait until you get three or four of these short quotes; then print them on a postcard along with the stylist's photo, and send them out to a "cold" list—the names of potential clients who aren't now your customers. The methods of obtaining lists are described in other promotions in this book. Suffice it to say, if you send out several hundred postcards it will cost you less than $100, and you'll make that up pretty quickly. The rest is then all new profit.

6 Chances are that all your stylists will want to have cards mailed out featuring them. They should understand, however, that whenever a client has a quotation used, she will have been promised free services and it will be up to the stylist she is complimenting to provide those free services. Stylists can't have their cake and eat it, too.

7 To be most effective, you should do a mailing to this cold list once a month or once every two months but no less frequently than that. Each time a mailing goes out, it should feature a different stylist. The effect will be cumulative. When the recipient is ready to go to a salon or change salons or try something new, she'll think, "This salon seems to have a lot of great people, and the testimonials are from local women (some of whom she may even know), so I think I give them a call." That's it. Success!

8 Another way to use this device is to advertise the whole salon. Your card will now say: "Here's what our clients say about our stylists at The Golden Hand Salon." Then you list the name of every stylist and a one, two, three, word "rave review" for each.

EACH TIME A MAILING GOES OUT, IT SHOULD FEATURE A DIFFERENT STYLIST. THE EFFECT WILL BE CUMULATIVE.

Often a client may be very satisfied with the work but not particularly verbal about it. If you need some quotes, ask her whether she was pleased with the service she received and specifically whether she was pleased enough to write a kind note. If you can't get an unsolicited testimonial, a solicited one will do.

While postcard advertising has been recommended here, if you have sufficient funds, this promotion can work beautifully in print advertising. One small ad a week in a local newspaper and featuring a different stylist each time on a rotating basis will positively have a cumulative effect. It will sink in that people doing the complimenting are legitimate people, and the stylists they are all raving about are happily congregated in your salon.

Watch what happens. Everyone loves recognition, so the stylists will clamor to be featured. But they're not the only ones. Once the newspaper advertising or the postcard messages start to take hold, you'll find clients actually asking to be quoted in future mailings. (When it gets to that point, you won't have to reward them with free services.) Starting now, pay particular attention to movie advertising. Observe the techniques. Absorb the techniques. You're not 20th Century Fox (yet), but you'll find that what works for them can work for you.

Beauty Crisis Hotline

One of the delicious little secrets of our industry is that the more beauty services consumers do by themselves at home, the more professional beauty service business we get from these very same consumers. Years ago when home perms were first invented, many people in the industry thought that permanent waving business in salons would collapse. Instead it grew as more and more consumers realized that getting perm results was not as easy as the ads promised. Then came home haircoloring, and to this day there are cosmetologists who violently oppose it, evidently oblivious to the fact that since the products themselves became available to consumers, haircoloring in salons has become the highest volume, highest profit chemical service in the history of our industry. And, of course, there are the countless women who perform their own nail services but panic when they wind up with a fungus or botched results.

The facts are plain for all to see. The more beauty services the consumer performs at home, the more messed up, botched up, fouled up results they'll achieve—and the more they'll look to the licensed salon and professional cosmetologist for refuge from the frizzed hair, green hair, messed up nails, and endless other beauty disasters they bring on themselves. We can turn these disasters to our advantage by offering to help these poor souls.

There are some promotions that are sort of "in and out." A little bit of publicity or advertising or signage, a short promotional period, and then it's over. This is not one of these promotions. This should be ongoing, and therefore you'll need ongoing promotion. A small ad will do the trick, but the key is that it must be an ongoing ad. It can even be placed in the classified section under an appropriate category such as Personal Services.

If you can afford more than a classified ad, you can take a one-column, two-inch ad. How much you can afford will, of course, be up to you. The more placements, the better. But it you can't have it run at least once a week on a continuing basis, pass this one by. If you elect to do it, your copy can read something like this:

> THE MORE BEAUTY SERVICES THE CONSUMER PERFORMS AT HOME, THE MORE THEY WILL LOOK TO THE PROFESSIONALS FOR REFUGE FROM BEAUTY DISASTERS THEY BRING ON THEMSELVES.

HELP!. . . . **for home perm problems, hair straightening problems, overprocessed hair, frizzies, haircolor corrective problems, nail fungus from wrapped or sculptured nails, etc.** . . . BEAUTY CRISIS HOTLINE **[Tel. No.]**

Be assured you'll get calls. Be prepared for the fact that many of them will want advice and nothing else. They may not be potential salon clients at this time, but the law of averages will be working for you. A certain amount of callers will never become salon clients, but a certain amount will. The key is that you must treat them all the same, with courtesy and professionalism.

Obviously you'd like every caller to become a salon client, but be careful not to make your wishes overt. If they think this is some sort of device to trick them into paying for your services in the salon, they'll back off. Always give people the best advice you can, but in all truthfulness and sincerity let them know that there's only a certain amount that can be done nonprofessionally and at home. You can put a Band-Aid on a scratch, but if it's a gash, you may need stitches at the doctor's.

Ideally, one person in the salon should be handling the Beauty Crisis Hotline. It must be a knowledgeable, intelligent person with excellent communication skills. Very often the best candidate is the salon owner. If that person is not immediately available when someone calls, the phone number must be taken, and the call returned as soon as possible.

This is one of those quiet, slow promotions that doesn't result in a huge influx of immediate business, but over time, it positively will build. Even those who don't have beauty problems will, by virtue of your ad campaign, be aware that you exist and that you can handle problem situations. You will get a reputation for expertise. People who don't have a problem today may have one months from today, and your name will come to mind. It's a slow build and a sure build. And, as everyone who has read about the tortoise and the hare knows, very often slow and sure wins the race.

THIS IS ONE OF THOSE QUIET, SLOW PROMOTIONS THAT DOESN'T RESULT IN A HUGE INFLUX OF IMMEDIATE BUSINESS, BUT OVER TIME, IT POSITIVELY WILL BUILD.

Book That Next Appointment During This Appointment

THE BEST THING A

CLIENT CAN POSSIBLY

DO FOR YOU IS TO

BOOK HER NEXT

APPOINTMENT ON

HER WAY OUT OF

THE SALON.

The time between the current appointment and the next appointment is always fraught with danger. It generally is four to six weeks, and during this time the client exposed to all sorts of influences that may induce her to try another salon for a change. Even if she intends to come back to your salon, she may decide to delay for another week or two. Both eventualities are bad for business. The best thing a client can possibly do for you is to book her next appointment on her way out of the salon.

This type of promotion succeeds or fails based on the abilities of your reception staff. As the client is paying her bill and preparing to take her leave, the critical moment arrives where she can be asked to book her next appointment. If the receptionist simply says, "Would you like to book your next appointment now?" the client will almost certainly say, "No, I'll just call in." So long. That's it. Now all we can do is hope that she returns. Very often she does, but very often she doesn't. Let's see if we can entice her to take out her little appointment book and make her next appointment on the spot.

Have little coupon/cards printed that say:

This entitles [<u>Name</u>] to a complimentary [<u>Product or Service</u>] when presented at her next appointment on [<u>Date</u>].

1 Decide on several products and/or services you can give away for free over the next several months. In products it can be anything that costs you a dollar or two maybe even three. Isn't it worth this amount to assure that that client will come back on a specific day some weeks from now? A $1 or $2 "insurance policy" that helps to "lock in" every client is about as good a way to spend your money as you possibly can.

If it is products you'll be using, sit down and talk turkey with your distributor, or whoever supplies the products. Explain that you'll be giving it away for free, so you've got to be able to buy it at absolute rock bottom. The distributor may even be induced to give you the products for free as part of their company's own sampling campaign.

But it need not only be products you can offer. Free services can be every bit as effective—a free "deep-conditioning," a free ten to fifteen minute scalp massage, a free waxing, a free mini-facial.

2 When the client is ready to leave, the receptionist now says, "Would you like to book your next appointment now? We're giving away a free [whatever] with advance appointments." Now the client will probably say, "Really? Hmm-m. Let me take a look at my schedule. OK, put me down for five weeks from today." Now she gets handed that card, appropriately filled in with the date of her appointment and the free product or service she is to receive. Note that a) She can't give the card to anyone else to redeem, because it's made out to her, b) a definite date is specified, and if she cancels her appointment, the card becomes null and void.

Why wouldn't a person book in advance? After all, she has absolutely nothing to lose. So she'll do it.

3 After a month or two you can either continue this promotion but with a different product or service to be given away, or you can discontinue it. It's best to continue it for several months just to get clients into the habit of booking in advance.

4 An alternative is to institute this promotion on and off periodically. When it's off and the client asks if there's any incentive to booking in advance, she can be told, "No not this time, but most of our clients like to have an advance booking just for the convenience of it." Some will book, some won't. Then when the promotion comes on again, everyone will flock to advance appointments all over again. Little by little they'll be trained, and they'll realize that whether they get a special incentive or not, it's very convenient to lock in an appointment. It can always be canceled or changed later on, so why not?

5 If you want to sweeten things still further so that a client will always book advance appointments whether your promotion is on or not, you can have a policy whereby if she consecutively books nine appointments in advance and keeps every one of those appointments, the tenth one will be free. Once she is locked into this program, she'll *want* to book in advance, and she'll *want* to keep each specified appointment unchanged.

YOU CAN HAVE A POLICY WHEREBY FOR EVERY NINE APPOINTMENTS A CLIENT BOOKS IN ADVANCE AND KEEPS, SHE GETS A TENTH ONE FOR FREE.

Remember, this is a promotion that does not depend on your stylists, colorists, estheticians, or nail artists. It depends on the reception staff, who are the first people clients see when they come in and the last they see on the way out. If the reception staff is good, if they're enthused about the idea and

NOTES

buy into it, it will work beautifully. If they already feel harassed, harried, and harangued and view this promotion as just one more chore, it won't fly. You've got to know your people; sit down and go through it thoroughly, and get them enthused.

Of course, enthusiasm will be a little easier to generate if they have some sort of incentive. Whatever the incentive is, it shouldn't be dependent on the actual number of advance appointments booked but rather on the advance appointments booked and kept. If the client is a no-show, it's also a no-incentive.

Remember, too, that if the people you want to do this seem uncooperative in carrying it out, that just might be your signal that maybe you need a different person and personality up there in front meeting, greeting, waving good-by—and booking advance appointments.

Free Instruction for
Home Skin Care

MISCELLANEOUS

It's taken a long time, but skin care in salons seems finally poised for a great leap forward. Nationwide, there are more esthetic schools than ever before, so there's an increasing pool of qualified estheticians. All salons opting for the day spa concept must include skin care services. Professional skin care companies are starting to advertise directly to consumers. Skin care is growing, no doubt about it. If you have a qualified esthetician on your staff, as well as appropriate appliances, and a full line of professional skin care products, the first skin-care clients you'll want to attract are those who are currently coming to you for hair services. One very excellent way to do this is to offer clients instruction on skin care *at home*. This is not as silly as it sounds. Professional skin care in the salon goes hand in hand with skin care at home. Here's how it works.

1 You start off by notifying clients who come to your salon right now that your qualified skin care person will be giving home skin care instruction to clients as a courtesy service.

2 Schedule the instruction sessions at a time when the salon is usually closed.

3 Don't overbook. A mere half-dozen appointments will assure that everyone gets individual attention. If you book more than that, have a qualified helper to supplement the services of the instructor.

4 Notify clients that participation is by registration only. They can't just pop in. If anyone asks to bring a friend, by all means let them. It's your chance to convert the friend into a client.

PROFESSIONAL SKIN CARE IN THE SALON GOES HAND IN HAND WITH SKIN CARE AT HOME.

NOTES

5 It is vital, crucial, absolutely necessary that clients bring all the skin care products with them that they normally use at home. This is your way of finding out what they're using, what's right, what's wrong, what should be substituted, what should be supplemented.

6 The sessions should begin with a short lecture that will establish the expertise of the esthetician. A discussion on the physiology of skin and what it needs to keep it in optimum condition is certainly in order. Then the discussion of home maintenance begins. The importance of cleansing, toning, moisturizing, and how to do them should be explained in general terms. The need for the appropriate skin care products must be discussed. If a client doesn't have these absolutely essential products, she can conceivably borrow them from her neighbor. But, of course, the preferred thing to do would be to purchase the appropriate products from you there and then. The return on your investment of time begins.

7 When everyone is into the beginning step of the regime, the instructor goes from client to client, giving individual instruction and tips and checking on whether the products being used are really the right ones, the appropriate ones, and up to the standards of the products you have for sale in the salon. Obviously many that will be inappropriate and/or below standard. In these cases, be assured that the clients will be happy to purchase the right products from you.

8 Follow this procedure over and over. As everyone explores each specific skin activity, go down the line advising, helping, adjusting, suggesting.

9 When there are individual skin care problems (for example, dry skin, oily skin, blackheads) you have another opportunity to prescribe products in your skin care line that will be appropriate.

10 All the while the instructor should exhibit her expertise by not only giving tips and suggestions but also by using biological and dermatological terms and techniques whenever possible. A simple illustration would be never to call a blackhead a blackhead. They are *comodones*.

11 When the instructional part of the session is completed, give a brief demonstration of what the typical, professional salon facial treatment performed by an esthetician consists. Trot out your machinery and your products. Explain what they do, how long it takes, and what the effects are. This will have everyone in the room mentally salivating. To have somebody doing it all for you instead of doing it yourself—ah, what a treat.

12 The next part is very optional but very advisable. The instructor should announce that total care of the skin should be a combination of using the right products in the right way at home *and* periodic and regular facial treatments in the salon. Announce that because you think this is so important—and because this particular class has been so interested, eager, and attentive—you're offering to give each of them a full salon facial treatment for *free*! That ought to elicit a spontaneous round of applause. Why is this so advisable? The clients are interested in skin care. They've been willing to devote time to it. They've been willing to buy some of your products in preference to their own. Their level of knowledge has been increased about skin, skin products, and the benefits of professional treatments. Some might automatically be ready to sign up for appointments. But the clincher will be a free "sample." How generous of you! Once those six hair care clients have gone through the lectures, the demonstrations, and the free treatments, they're yours.

Obviously, six clients exposed to professional skin care instruction and treatment are not very many. But that's only one session. If you did this once a week for a couple of months, you'll have reached about fifty clients. The numbers add up very quickly. And remember that while they won't all book for steady salon facial treatments, many of them will, and that's all found business. A good percentage of the rest will be buying your skin care products rather than grocery store brands because they were specifically prescribed. That's also found business. The cost of this kind of promotion is virtually nothing in terms of dollars. The investment will be in time, and it will be an investment that pays off.

Finally, remember that all of the above applies to makeup, as well. Got a competent makeup artist? Separate and apart from the skin care sessions, you can have makeup sessions. Now you'll really be cookin'. Skin care sessions, makeup sessions, product sales, treatment sales, makeup lessons—property handled, you'll probably have to start looking for an additional esthetician and/or makeup artist to handle all the new business. Nice, eh?

THE COST OF THIS KIND OF PROMOTION IS VIRTUALLY NOTHING IN TERMS OF DOLLARS.

Promo 101 | Letters of Recommendation Build Business without Discounts

MISCELLANEOUS

We all know that the best advertising is word of mouth. You do a great cut, color, or perm on a client, and she's so thrilled that she tells her friends of her great new "find," and Such-and-Such Salon. Sometimes it happens that your salon's clients are pleased, they come back for repeat appointments and they love you, but they may simply neglect to talk up the work you do. These are clients who would be happy to recommend you, but just don't think about doing it. There's a device you can use to encourage them. Very simply, it's a "Letter of Recommendation."

1 Right across the top of an $8\frac{1}{2} \times 11$ piece of stationery, big and bold, you print LETTER OF RECOMMENDATION. Then you write some simple copy, something like this:

> To Whom It May Concern: We, the undersigned beautiful people would like to recommend the Such-and-Such Salon to all who have wondered about their present hairstyle, color, hair condition, or significant other's opinion. We don't have to wonder. We know we're in good hands at the Such-and-Such Salon.

2 Have two or three dozen clients sign this Letter of Recommendation, and then end it with your own statement, something like:

> We love our clients and we appreciate them. So we stay up-to-date on all the latest styles, trends, techniques, and products to feel confident that we are always giving them the best that they can get so they can be the best they can be. Please give us a call. We'd love to welcome you into our large family of friends and clients.

NOTES

3 You can't get much more basic than that. Take that letter to a printer and run off a few hundred copies. Mail them out to a local mailing list, or stand in a local shopping center (if other merchants don't object) and simply hand them out.

When people in your immediate area get this letter, you can be sure they'll go through the names to see if they know anyone. If they find a friend, it's bound to result in conversation and a recommendation for your salon. Even if they don't know anyone who signs the letter, it has a ring of truth and sincerity, and chances are many will call to give your salon a try.

One of the particularly nice aspects of this specific promotion is that it doesn't offer any discounts. It just asks for people to come in because their friends and neighbors recommend it. Obviously, you can attach special offers and discounts if you'd like, but they're really not necessary. The Letter of Recommendation will stand on its own.

And Now . . .

The WELCOME sign is out at the portals of promotion. You've taken an important step. You've read 101 different promotions. You've evaluated them. You've learned techniques. You've gotten ideas. *Don't stop now.* The next step is to get affirmation. Ask people who have read the book to give you feedback and see what promotions you agree would be the appropriate ones for your salon.

How many promotions should you plan on doing? I can't give you a hard and fast recommendation. I know salons that promote twelve months a year, a different promotion each month. If you're not used to this kind of promotional schedule, don't even think about doing it. The worst possible thing you can do is bite off more than you can chew. On the other hand, you won't want to pick only one promotion. You really want to have a promotional schedule for the entire year, and one per year won't make it. Two promotions a year aren't enough, either. The salon and the staff will have too much time to droop between promotions.

My suggestion, if you're not used to promoting, is to start with four, one every three months. If you'd like, it can be one every season.

Are you used to promoting? Have you done it successfully in the past? Maybe you'll want to do six a year, one every other month. It's up to you.

Of course, if you are a heavily promotional salon, go to it. One promotion each month will keep you in a constant state of promotional activity and growth. Even at one a month you'll find enough promotions in this book to keep you busy for years!

Let's assume you're going to do four promotions in the next year. The hard part is going to be which four. After all, you have 101 to choose from. It won't be 101 after you compare the promotions you and your "counselors" agree on. But it will be lots, many more than you actually need. Here again there are so many varieties in the personalities and talents of salons that it's impossible to advise you on which specific one to start with. But you'll *know*, you really will. You know your neighborhood, your clientele, your competition, your staff. You'll know which promotion will be the easiest to start off with.

One thing you must positively do is schedule a meeting with your staff to keep everyone in the salon totally informed. Distributor and manufacturer sales reps call on your salon. Be assured that whenever they come out with a new promotion, they attend a sales meeting where all aspects of the promotion are explained. The boss, distributor, regional manager, or whoever enthusiastically presents the promotion and motivates them to give it their all so that all may benefit. You must do the same. It's not hard, but it does involve some advance thought, planning, and preparation so that you can present it with the maximum amount of knowledge and enthusiasm.

Try to pick a time when people are reasonably "up" instead of tired and worn out at the end of a busy Friday. Serve refreshments. Champagne wouldn't be out of order.

You've discovered promotions in this book that don't actually involve any of the employees. They are promotions only you will execute to attract new clients. Stylists simply have to properly take care of these clients as they are drawn in. Just because stylists don't have to make any special preparations up front doesn't mean you don't have to keep them informed. All promotions work best when there is salon teamwork—and there can't be teamwork without proper information and communication.

If a promotion you choose does indeed entail the complete involvement and cooperation of your staff, you should explain every aspect of the promotion, what exactly you are going to do, what will be expected of them, and how they and the salon will benefit. If any of the staff members were involved in selecting the promotion or preparing for it, have them participate in your presentation in terms of telling why they like it, why they think it will be a success.

Now you need a calendar and a yellow pad. Go back to the page in the book that has the promotion you're going to start with. Make a list of the things you're going to do, whom to contact. A printer? A sign painter? A newspaper beauty editor? Your distributor? What will you need and when will you need it? Write all this down on the yellow pad. After going through all 101 promotions in this book, thoughts will flow out of your brain and onto the paper. If you need more ideas, go through the book again. This time you can do it more quickly. Ideas, suggestions, things to do will jump out at you from promotions other than the ones you've chosen. Put down a deadline for each ask that has to be done. But don't put yourself under too much pressure. Give yourself comfortable lead times.

The most successful promotion is one where everybody wins. Clients get better service and value. The staff gets increased income. The salon owner benefits financially. And the salon itself has greater morale and can fund more educational programs, advertising, and, yes, more promotions. What a worthy goal to aspire to: an activity where *everyone* connected with the salon benefits.

One of the loveliest parts of the whole plan is that it's a goal that's easy to achieve. It's there for the asking and the doing. It's within everyone's reach—everyone's. All that remains is to take a deep breath, put a smile on your face, and just do it.

Congratulations, my colleague, and good luck.